Professional Praise

Mia Redrick is a master! She shines a bright light on mothers' tendencies to ignore their own needs and to put themselves at the bottom of their own priority lists. Not content with raising our awareness, she offers innovative, practical solutions for weaving self-care into any moms daily life. Every busy mother must read this book.

Delia Chiaramonte, M.D.
www.insightmedicalconsultants.com

Why a mother's self-care is relevant today

Many women find themselves overwhelmed, lost, depressed, anxious, resigned to a sad notion that their mental and emotional state is the price of motherhood.

Their own well-being often takes the backseat to their children's piano, soccer and school, or to their husbands' power meetings or personal progress. While these things are all important in managing, nurturing and caring for family, many women lose their way and forget to care for themselves.

As a mother I know that a mom's course can be very winding and complicated, but as a psychiatrist I am constantly confronted with the unsettling physical and mental health complications that result from getting stressed OUT and lost along the way.

While the bottom line is true - stress cannot be erased however; with the right tools, it can surely be managed.

Way to go Mom Coach, Mia Redrick! You have clearly straightened a path on this course that can be navigated with ease and some really great souvenirs on the journey.

Your conceptualization of a mother's self-care as a tool for stress management and living life to its fullest is not only innovative and relevant to today's mothers, it is long overdue.

Dr. Melva Green MD, MPH, MBA
www.drmelvagreen.com

I have known Mia for about nine years now. We met through Mocha Moms, now known as a nationally recognized group for stay-at-home moms of color. Mia was the president and I worked under her supporting community outreach. Mia and I never lost touch. Through various stages of motherhood, Mia has always found calm for herself and other moms around her. She is constantly learning. She is never without a book title or a blurb that she has read that would be beneficial to me as a 'mom' friend. Mia's own book is long overdue! Her positive attitude and approach to life problems as a mother is unprecedented. She has coached me through three or four moves, job changes, death in the family, starting a new business, grandparent involvement, and family relationships and how they affect you as a mother. Mia puts a personal touch to each life problem I have shared with her. She is never without a hilarious story that puts your issue into perspective! I trust Mia; depend on Mia, and most of all love Mia!

This book, which I hope turns into a series, will be a resource for any mother who needs support.

All the best! Much love and success,
Michelle Cummings
President/Owner of Babysitease.com

I am a recent subscriber to Finding Definitions. As a woman, mom of five beautiful children and the President/CEO of my own company and a non-profit corporation, Finding Definitions has been for me the coach's coach, both inspiring and motivating me to balance the many roles in my life.

Shametra L. Thomas President/CEO
Reinventing Coaching & Consulting
The Inspire Project

Excerpts from Letters to Mia

Having my first child fairly young, it seems we've always had kids to think about. I set my dreams aside to do what I thought necessary for their success and happiness. Consequently, my personal wants really didn't exist. The first time Mia asked me "What do you want for you?" I was totally stumped. Through the coaching process, I'm learning how to answer that question while being true to myself, without feeling guilty, or sacrificing what I want for my family. My reflection is changing before my very eyes, and I have Mia to thank.

– Miameesha Clapp

The coaching process is really underrated. Mia, I've gained so much and accomplished things that would've taken years to accomplish, if I could have accomplished them at all. When I worked, I would set goals, make lists of things to do to achieve the goals on a daily basis, cross off the things I had accomplished (which really made me feel good) and talked with my managers and other colleagues about other things I wanted to accomplish and strategies to do those things. The coaching process has allowed me to understand that these practices shouldn't change if I continue to want to accomplish things. Well, at-home moms don't necessarily have the colleagues and don't have the managers to keep you on point, although we have the daily activities and we have loads of things that need to get done. So I feel the coaching process is good in that it gives me the structure to continue to set goals, plan out the steps to achieve those goals and to help in strategizing my next steps. The coaching process has given me tools and processes to use in lieu of having the structure of a conventional workplace, and these tools and processes will help me to continue to be successful at what I wish to do.

– Tracey from Pennsylvania

Ever since I received your first assignment, I have been thinking about the questions you asked, "What's important to you and what will make you happy?" I've really been doing some soul searching and have decided to make a few changes. One was resigning from a long term volunteer commitment. Honestly, I think I should have been gone a long time ago but... I'm also re-examining everything else I'm involved in and really trying to determine if I'm doing what I need to be doing at this time in my life.

I know I'm going on and on, but I just wanted you to know that I credit my mom coaching experience with you for prompting the majority of the change that's going on in my life. I realize it was only one session; but, honestly my thought life started to change the minute I read your questions.

I guess what I'm trying to say is THANK YOU SO VERY MUCH! I truly appreciate you!

– Shawanda from Georgia

I want to take this opportunity to say thank you. Your advice is so timely. I am 40 years old with a 3-year-old daughter and 5-year-old son and no siblings of my own. Without younger siblings I didn't have any practice in day-to-day childcare. Changing a diaper was new for me. I am doing 'on the job training' everyday. Not to mention that my husband had a stroke earlier this year; so, I am a married person who has to function as a single person. I am not complaining, but it sure takes several strategies. One I recently enjoyed was taking the children to Taco Bell and ordering through the drive-thru and picking it up inside as a dine-in order. This kept my children from jumping around while I waited in line to order. It worked like a charm.

– God Bless You,
Rostine Webb

TIME FOR ME

MIA REDRICK
The Mom Strategist

Finding Definitions, LLC
P. O. Box 68045
Baltimore, MD 21215

Library of Congress Cataloging-in-Publication Data

Time for mom-me: 5 Essential Self-care Strategies for Mothers
Second Edition: November 2010

ISBN 9780979627309 (tradepaper)

- Self-Help I. Redrick, Mia
- Parenting

Library of Congress Control Number: 2008900961

Printed in the United States of America by Lightning Source Inc.

For information about special discounts for bulk purchases, please contact Finding Definitions Sales at 1-866-226-2607 or info@findingdefinitions.com.

Contents

Acknowledgements

Taking the steps to pursue your dreams is a daily decision. The support, encouragement and love of others often allow our dreams to take flight. I am very fortunate to have great wingmen and wing moms. They are:

Patrick (my hubby): Thank you for understanding my vision. I appreciate the commitments that you have made to help me make my dreams possible. I am blessed to have your support and love. Big hugs and kisses, and loads of love!

Patrick, Alexandra and Matthew: You are the best children ever! I appreciate all of your advice, support, and understanding that writing a book takes commitment.

I love you all.

Mom and Dad: Mom, thank you for teaching me the importance of self-care from the beginning of my early days as a mom. Dad, I appreciate your example that everything is possible. I love you both.

James, Michelle and Taylor and Ashley: James you are the funniest brother around. You always make me smile. Michelle, I am blessed to have you as my sister-in-law. Taylor and Ashley, you are the best nieces in the world.

Tillena: You are so smart and thank you for lending me your ear after 10:00pm. I love you Kevin, Nia and Jada.

Coach T.: You are the best coach in the Universe. You have always made requests of me that have allowed me to own my best and reach for more. Love Ya.

Doc. Delia and Melva: You are the best running buddies a girl could ask for. You are terrific doctors. I am glad that the world finally knows. I appreciate your expertise, wisdom and support.

Altscher: You are a great biz consultant. I respect you a great deal. "You are hired." Thank you for your faith in me.

Miameesha and Yamisi, my administrative team: Thank you both for all your support and hard work.

You are the best. I could not have gotten this far without the two of you.

Leonard S.: My Web guy, thank you for always translating the technical.

Michelle C.: Your support always touches me and reminds me of the benefit of great friendships.

Dr. Hug: You are so smart and supportive. You teach me so much!

Shawn S.: I appreciate your friendship and encouragement.

Phil Wilkins: Thank you for always sharing. Your example of great business has taught me a lot. I am listening.

Darryl Mobley: I love your example of creating a business that supports families. Thank you for believing in me.

Wayne: Thank you for the beautiful photos for this book. Thanks for sharing the beautiful backdrop of nature with me.

Audrey: I love the way you style my hair. You are very talented and the best conversationalist around.

Linda at Wordpros and Anne Henslee: You are the best editors in the world. Thank you for excelling in the English language.

Robin: Thank you for always listening to my zany ideas and never laughing. You are a great photographer. Thank you for sharing your gifts with me. I appreciate you.

Andrea B.: Everyone needs an honest friend. You are mine.

Lydia W.: You are the best publicist in town. Thank you.

Carolyn: I love the book layout. You are a terrific pro.

Last but not least, my clients. Thank you all for validating that Mom coaching is essential to a woman's growth and development. I respect all of you and have learned from your willingness to be your personal best.

Remember to always…
Live Fully.
Mia

Foreword

The Coaching Expert for Moms Arrives

Our world runs in a high-stress and fast-pace mode. We keep asking the question, "Where is the time going?" noticing how quickly our lives are moving. When a woman becomes a mother, her world changes in many ways, and it seems to move at an even faster pace. Yet, during the time of motherhood, women often feel their world has slowed and stopped because of the amount of change that happens.

With motherhood being perhaps the most significant phase in the lives of many women, we cannot overlook this time and what happens to women as they become mothers. As a woman moves into motherhood she goes through change, expansion, fear, growth, and even shrinkage. She gets focused on her baby and often loses touch with who she is and what her own personal needs are. Everything she reads and hears is about taking great care of her baby. We have little to say as a culture about how the mother can care for herself.

Just pick up a magazine for expectant moms. It is filled with reviews and ads for the best baby products. Where are the products that care for and nurture the expectant mother? Instead, we educate the mother on what to expect during pregnancy, how to care for her baby, and how to be a great parent. We ignore the fact that this phase of her life is going to be a stress-filled roller-coaster and instead show her pictures of happy, smiling babies.

Mothers still remain the chief care-givers even today. Yet we don't provide self-help for those care-givers. Did we forget that being a mother is not just about enjoying the first smiles, the rollovers, crawls and runs? There is so much more to being a mother.

When I was growing up, I remember hearing the expression, "a mother's work is never done." I think this holds true. I see mothers trying to wash the floor while their child is tossing goldfish crackers on the floor. The mother's job is to remain happy and calm and to just continue to smile, pick up the goldfish and keep washing the floor.

Mom's days are long, filled with many tasks and, depending on the support of her partner, she may not have the external support systems she needs. I always wonder how my mom got up each day tirelessly and continued to smile when she often felt under-appreciated.

My dad went to work and pretty much knew his daily calendar and job tasks. My mom on the other hand never really knew how her day would unfold. Would the school nurse call saying she had to come pick one of us up? Would we bring friends home to mess up the house she had cleaned? Would it rain and we track mud all over the house?

Working moms have long days too, and most of them report feeling tired and drained. They don't get a lot of positive accolades for mothering and don't get much positive feedback on the job they are doing as a mother. The job of mothering doesn't have certain specific hours and is tireless work. There is no yearly performance review filled with praise and no raise or bonus incentive.

Stop and look at the role of a mother and you will realize that mothers influence our course. Think about your own life and how your mother influenced you. Isn't it logical to help mothers to live their best, most vibrant and fulfilling lives? When mothers are feeling great, are caring for themselves and not burned out, then they are truly a gift to the family and to society. And this book will help them in that regard.

I believe this book is long overdue and cherish the fact it has finally arrived! Mia's perspective on self-care for moms is refreshing and much needed. Mia is the credible expert on this topic. As a mom of three children she speaks to the heart of mothers everywhere who voice the question that mothers are constantly toying with inside: What is the meaning of my life?

She then gives moms a sense of what they are experiencing during the wonderful stage of motherhood so they better understand themselves and their new situation. There is real value in knowing you are not alone and that others are going through what you are in this phase of life. This sense of knowing what you are experiencing is to be expected, and knowing you are joined by other women can really give you self peace.

One of the best ways for mothers to get support, insight, inspiration, advice and answers is through the coaching process. Coaching provides moms with the opportunity to explore their own feelings about life and to help them get back their sense of humor in dealing with day-to-day parenting issues. Coaching is like having your own personal support system. The support systems of women in neighborhoods getting together to have coffee and chat about their children are long gone to most of us. Moms are busy working and trying to do things on their own without outside support systems.

Through the coaching approach in this book, you will learn to take better care of yourself and create strategies to create inner peace and calm, to recharge and refresh yourself. You will feel more power, greater self-confidence and will be happier in your role of being a mom.

What I really enjoyed in this book is how Mia asks moms the right, powerful coaching questions. Mia approaches the moms from her position as a coaching expert. She brings her extraordinary coaching skills and tools right into the book. Mia knows the right questions that will unveil a mother's understanding. As a mom herself, she relates to the personal challenges that mothers face. She knows what moms must overcome to benefit both themselves as well as their families.

As a trainer of thousands of professional coaches around the world and as a parent coach, I have believed that a great coaching book was needed just for moms. I was delighted when Mia told me she was writing this book!

It takes this powerful coach who also has mom experience to come forth with her personal perspective on mom coaching. It is evident Mia cares deeply about impacting other mothers' lives in a very positive and lasting way. It is time that we have moms learn what works for their personal growth and evolution. Clearly, Mia understands moms. Through her company, she provides the resources for mothers to live higher quality lives instead of high quantity living.

As you read this book, you will know that the only selfish act is not to love yourself. Understand that the more you love yourself the better you are able to extend that love to others.

Terri Levine, Ph.D.
The Guru of Coaching[SM]
www.CoachInstitute.com

How to use Finding Time for mom-Me

Finding Time for mom-Me was created as a resource for anyone who defines herself as a mom.

To make the most of reading this book I encourage you to answer the questions honestly, quietly and reflectively. The purpose of the assignments is to get you to think about your life and to aid you in altering the habits, routines, relationships, processes and infrastructure that prevent you from living the life about which you dream.

This book was written with an understanding of the busyness of a mother's life. It is designed as a simple but powerful resource to help move moms toward actions that will assist them in recreating and renegotiating a life that is rich, fulfilling and meaningful.

Before beginning any chapter, I recommend that you close your eyes and empty your thoughts, stress and schedule for the day. Take a deep breath and breathe in and out slowly to relax your body. Take a minimum of 15 minutes each day to read this book and complete the assignments and practices. Remember to focus only on you while reading this book.

At the end of each chapter, there is an affirmation where you can sign and date, *"I took an action for me today and it felt great!"* The goal is to help you build the muscle of doing something to improve your life every day by taking small steps. Be sure to use the journal at the end of each chapter to record your thoughts.

Throughout the chapters there are various assignments and practices. Although you might want to skip ahead to the next chapter, if this is your first time reading this book, it is recommended that you completely finish one chapter before moving to the next. All of the chapters are building blocks to help you redevelop patterns that will help you move forward easily.

Connect to a community for accountability

- ✔ Join with your local mom's group.

- ✔ Start a timeformom-me group dedicated to being support for one another. Go to www.timeformom-me.com to learn how.

- ✔ Partner with your friends, co-workers, or family members who are moms.

We want to hear from you. Share your insights with us at info@timeformom-me.com. Go to www.timeformom-me.com, our online community to meet other moms, share ideas or learn how other mothers are self-accomplishing as moms.

More importantly, just get started on this terrific journey to self-definition. I am excited for you, and I will be there every step of the way.

Live Fully,
Mia

Affirmation

I took an action for me today and it felt great!

____

(Your Signature)

How to use Finding Time for mom-Me Journal Sections

Congratulations on your purchase of Finding Time for mom-Me, 5 Essential Strategies for A Mother's Self-Care and on making the decision to commit to yourself. This journal section serves as a guide to help you enhance the current blueprint for your life. As moms, we become so busy taking care of our families that we forget to listen to our own voice. This journal will help you find your voice and discover who you are again.

Journaling daily will help you keep a written record of your life. As moms, we become so busy with the demands of family, home and work that we forget to consider how we feel. This journal was created specifically for you to write about your life as mom. Each day, take fifteen minutes to record how you feel about your life. Write about your thoughts and feelings about yourself, your day or anything that you wish. If you get stuck, I have created a list of questions for each chapter to consider when journaling in the back of each chapter. Choose one or two questions from my list to help you get started. I encourage you to add your own questions to this list.

The goal is for you to begin to hear from yourself again. I want you to have a written record of the things that you want to keep in your life and the things that you want change. Taking the time everyday to hear your inner desires is the best way to Live Fully.

Suggested Journal Questions:

1. What do I want for my life? Who am I? What do I like about my life? What do I want to change? What is working? What is not?

2. How do I feel? What in my life brings me the greatest joy? What brings me the least enjoyment? What do I do for pleasure? How do I relax?

3. When was the last time I reflected on me? How do I renew and rejuvenate myself? When was the last time I was still?

4. Do I feel powerful or powerless? Why? What are my boundaries? Do I exercise choice in my life? Do I trust myself?

5. Why do I love me? What am I grateful for? What are my priorities? What can I celebrate about me? Do I show myself love? How? When?

6. What is my life telling me? What do I need to get rid of?

7. What opportunities are around me? What is my dream? What is my purpose?

8. When was the last time I was alone? How much rest do I need? When was the last time I cried? When was the last time I laughed?

9. What makes me smile? Am I dancing to the music of life?

10. Do I enjoy my friendships? What kind of friend am I? When was the last time I helped someone in need?

My Intention in Writing This Book

My intention in writing this book is to create both dialogue and a support community among women as mothers that address the realities of being a mom as they relate to self-definition. My goal is to provide you with strategies and solutions that will set you on a path to find meaningful ways to incorporate yourself into your life as mommy.

Considering the steps that a mother must take are essential for any mom who wants more out of her life, whether a home-schooler, work-at-home, or stay-at-home professional. Moms all want the same things – happy families. We also want to be happy ourselves.

To that end, I did a simple search on Amazon.com. I searched for book titles on "mom self-care" and found 72 book titles. I then searched the title "mom support" and located 1,315 books. Next, I searched "parenting" and found 47,824 titles, while "parenting support" had just 2,067 titles. Finally, I searched "parenting self-care" and discovered 158 titles. From this unscientific Amazon database search, we can see that more content is needed to help parents navigate their own care in this life of parenting.

I found that the personal happiness of Mom directly contributes to a happy family.

If you were asked to write your personal entry in the Webster's Dictionary today of your definition of mom and the definition of me, what would you say? Perhaps your definitions might say something like this:

Mom: (mom)
Noun
Definition: woman who loves, nurtures, rears, protects, teaches child
Synonym: ME

Me: (me)
Pronoun
Definition: woman who loves, nurtures, rears,

protects,teaches child
Synonym: Mom

Your turn! Write your definition of Mom and then your definition of "Me."

Mom (mom)
Noun
Definition:
Synonym:

Me (me)
Pronoun
Definition:
Synonym:

What are your observations about your definition? Are you surprised by the level of challenge that this simple exercise caused you?

"A mother is a person who seeing there are only four pieces of pie for five people, promptly announces she never did care for pie"
– Tenneva Jordan

I created this program to help mothers expand their limited definition of themselves as mothers. My goal is to challenge moms to live fully, be healthy, dream big and personally grow in their own lives while being a great mom. While there is no one-size-fits-all strategy for self-care, I propose throughout this book the essential guidelines for placing yourself at the top of the list.

I decided to write this book because I have read countless books on helping mothers find balance. The truth of the matter is that balance is not something we find; it is something we create.

Live Fully,
Mia

What is Finding Definitions?

Time for mom-Me was created to teach mothers that self-care is not negotiable but necessary to be the best person possible. As a mom coach strategist, I ask my clients the tough questions to unlock their answers for a happier life. Through a series of my questions you will better be able to identify who you are and what you want for your life.

Finding Definitions helps mothers

Find Time . . . . To Self Accomplish

Find Balance . . . . To Enjoy Each Day

Find Meaning. . . . . To Listen to Your Voice

Find Connection . . To Establish Supportive Networks

Find You. . . . . To Discover Who You Are

Find Gratitude . . . . To Acknowledge
What Makes You Happy

This is not an ordinary book for mothers. Finding Time for mom-Me is specifically designed for mothers to encourage them to be honest about their lives. I want moms to Reflect, Release, Renew and Resolve. It is my hope that this book and the journaling section will aid you in creating the life you want.

Use it daily and challenge yourself with the tough questions about the quality of your life. Visit my website at www.findingdefinitions.com for additional resources on assigning meaning to your life as mom.

Thank you in advance for making you a priority.

Live Fully,
Mia

CHAPTER 1

Blueprint of Motherhood

Being a mother changes everything!

When we become mothers, it changes our routines, patterns and the way we love. Never before did we know it was possible to love fingertips and toes. As we evolve as mothers, we find it difficult and less important to continue to do for ourselves as we did before we had children.

It was never our intention to lose ourselves; it just happened as part of this new set of expectations, obligations and the abyss of the unknown. We would have been ahead of the curve if we really understood what we were reading in those parenting books that told us to take all the naps we could and to maintain a personal routine after having a baby.

In fact, motherhood is like being thrown a curve ball. Just when you think you know what you are doing, you find yourself somewhere else. I remember preparing for my first public outing alone with my son, Patrick. I had the best stroller, the best car seat and a fully packed baby bag. I was ready! The curve ball came when I got to the mall and walked among the insensitive spectators – the ones who want to touch your newborn's face and fingers. I knew they were out there. I just did not know that I would have to address them right away. Another curve ball came when I undressed the baby in very little space in a public bathroom. I was prepared with props, but not prepared emotionally to hear the five toilets flush while I changed my newborn. Finally, the last curve ball hit me when I attempted to close my designer stroller. I had not practiced the taking down. This was unnerving and required me to ask many strangers for help and assistance. I quickly learned that motherhood is all about handling the curve balls.

"Motherhood has a very humanizing effect.
Everything gets reduced to essentials"
– Meryl Streep

My mother said to me soon after my son was born that being a mother is what you do, not who you are. I remember thinking at the time that this was insane. Being a mother is who I am now. I am a mother. I have waited all my life for this moment, and now I am a mother. But my own mother was absolutely right. Being a mother is playing a role, a role that many women developed from their earliest experiences.

What adjectives do you use to describe a mother?

Being a mom describes one aspect of who I am as a woman. What my mom wanted me to understand from the beginning is that being a good mom has much to do with your ability to be good to yourself.

And there are many ways to be good to yourself.

As women, we learn from the mothers in our lives how to and how not to mom. Many times when I am conducting a workshop, I ask the participants to look for similarities between themselves and their mothers. Many of us pick up behaviors and attitudes from our mothers without thinking about it. I call this our mothering script or blueprint.

"All women become like their mothers. That is their tragedy. No man does. That's his."
– Oscar Wilde
(The Importance of Being Earnest, 1895)

What is your mom-Me script?

Have you placed limitations on what you can achieve because you are a mom? Does your life as mom resemble your mother's? Are you unsure how you have created the life you have gotten? Let's explore your mommy script. In order to accurately assess your current mommy behaviors, complete the following exercise being completely honest. Use a journal to detail your responses.

Mom-Me Assessment

Consider the following:

1. Growing up, I best remember my mother's parenting styles as (i.e. controlling, permissive, detached, etc...).

2. I can best describe my parenting style as (i.e. controlling, permissive, detached, etc…).

3. How has my mother's style of parenting influenced me? Do I see any similarities or striking differences based on my childhood experiences?

4. Growing up, my mother (always, occasionally, never) found time for herself. When she did, she would…

5. Or…She never found time because…

6. As a mom, I (always, occasionally, never) find time for myself. When I do, I…

7. Or…I never find time because…

8. Do I see any similarities or differences based on my childhood experiences?

9. I loved the way my mother used to…

10. How has that affected my parenting style? Do I do the same thing now?

11. I did not like the way she used to…

12. How has this influenced my parenting style?

13. Do I do the same, total opposite, or somewhere in between?

14. What questions would I like to add about my mom "me" script?

A mothering script many times causes us to continue to do the same things our mom did with and to us when we were little. Many young women begin by using their mother's example as the basis of their own family life. Is this you? Maybe your mother gave everything to her children and left nothing for herself.

The purpose of raising these issues is to make you conscious of why you "mom" the way that you do.

One of the best ways to understand your life is by making powerful observations and by asking yourself the right questions about your habits, thoughts and feelings. Throughout this book I will help you make those observations and ask you the right questions to unlock the answers inside of you.

Marisa's mom, Kelly, worked part-time and was always home for the children by the time they got out of school. She was a happy woman but always made sure that profes-

sional and personal commitments did not interfere with her time with the children. She volunteered at church a couple of times a week and kept her schedule clear for the children's commitments.

Marisa, now a mother herself, followed the same routine. She liked her life but had no idea why she operated the way she did. She came to me because she wanted to start a business and could not see how it was possible.

The Silent War

There is a silent war in motherhood that threatens the uncultivated self. This silent war is a lack of self-care and it operates like one big muscle. If we fail to exercise, it becomes flabby and out of shape.

For mothers, a lack of self-care surfaces slowly and quietly. We can no longer identify what we like to read or movies we enjoy seeing. Sometimes we are too busy to add our own needs to the list. We are no longer multitasking as moms; we are mega-tasking moms.

"Any mother could perform the jobs of several air traffic controllers with ease"
– Lisa Alther

This silent war of motherhood defeats us when we stop knowing ourselves. For most women, it is a gradual process of developing habits and thoughts that make us feel that we are selfish for wanting to have hobbies, quality friendships, dates with our husbands, and careers. Logic dictates that it is impossible to do all of these things and be a great mom.

The silent war often goes on for years until one day we realize that we have become unfamiliar with the person we once were. We are unable to identify the simple things, such as our favorite restaurants, outfits that look best on our bodies, music we love, movies we want to see, or places we love to visit.

What would you add to this list?

I have spoken with many moms regarding this process of silently fading away. The irony for many is while our lives are fading, our children are thriving. Somehow as moms we manage to coordinate the children's lives to include schooling, extracurricular activities, healthy meals, play-time, hobbies, and play dates for growing friendships, but we fail to create any of these for ourselves. We have an internal war that says *"Not now." "There isn't enough time or resources." "Just wait until… they graduate, I go back to work, the summer comes,"* or whatever your reason is for putting yourself on hold.

Is this you? Are you making these false assumptions of motherhood?

The Assumptions of Motherhood

FALSE ASSUMPTIONS	TRUE ASSUMPTIONS
You will no longer need friends the way you did when you were in high school.	Motherhood requires rich and meaningful relationships with friends who fuel and support you. Friendships help validate who we are as mothers.
You don't have time for ("you.")	There is plenty of time for you.
Personal growth is not important	Your personal growth makes you a better parent.
Self-care takes a lot of time	Self-care is a mindset that establishes your life with you at the top of the list. Understand that if you take care of you, you will be better able to care for others.
Once you have children your life doesn't mean the same.	Yes, it is true that having children changes your life. However, having children does not mean that your life doesn't count. As a mom you probably teach your children to value their personal existence. What about you? What does your life mean?

CHAPTER 2

Personal Growth

Think of yourself as your favorite piece of jewelry. What does your favorite piece of jewelry look like when it is dirty? Does it shine or reflect light? The same is true with our lives when we fail to polish, buff or enhance ourselves by personally growing. We stop shining, singing, and reflecting the light that is inside of us. That may mean we are not as happy or fulfilled as we can be.

As mothers we nurture the needs and wants of our family members and leave very little for ourselves. As a result, we stop growing; we stop knowing ourselves. Remember when you used to accomplish something different for yourself every day? Remember how you felt? When we stop doing the little things for ourselves that we once did – like pursuing hobbies, making friends and looking our best – we stop knowing how to accomplish those things.

Personal growth is cultivating yourself in ways that leave you changed for the better. When we take the time to look our best, we change the way we see ourselves and we change how others see us. When we take the time to create meaningful adult relationships, we are supported, validated and provided with a network of resources for ourselves.

What is Personal Growth for Moms?

Personal growth is recognizing that we have the capacity to be more of who we are. It is understanding that each of us has the ability to grow, enhance and evolve as a woman. When we grow, we are able to enrich those around us as well as ourselves. We are able to work toward our goal of personal excellence and expand our gifts, talents and potential.

As mothers, many times we feel stifled by our busy schedules or unscheduled interruptions, like sick children, tantrums or a host of other mommy issues.

Whether you are the mother of multiples, preschoolers or school-aged children, your days may not always go according to plan. To ensure your success you have to have a mindset that is specific about what you are trying to accomplish – for you – every day.

As moms, we sometimes stop growing personally because of the distractions of life. Finding ways to balance the noise of work, home commitments, family and self seems daunting. Most times the transitions or unscheduled interruptions get us off track and result in our creating habits which are not helpful. Though it might be challenging to self-accomplish during the early weeks after having children, you should begin to create a routine that includes you as soon as possible. Some call it striking personal balance, but I call it managing personal transition. Finding personal time, particularly after having a new child or transitioning back to work, is the key to feeling good about our lives.

The Benefits of Personal Growth

✓ **To be happy with your life**. Happy mothers make happy families.

✓ **To reclaim the beautiful art of cultivating the self**. Moms! Reclaim YOU!

✓ **Recognizing that we can always evolve, even as mothers**. Our children aren't the only ones who can grow.

✓ **To increase our ability to have meaningful relationships with others**. Make connections that improve your life.

✓ **To provide ourselves with creative outlets that allow us to share ourselves with the world**. Growing is not about checking off a list of things to do, but instead doing something as an expression of joy or self-worth.

✓ **Growing means we are moving to enhance our life, not growing to reach a specific destination**. Make time to enjoy the journey.

✓ **Growing means showing yourself love**. You deserve love, don't you? Don't forget the importance of treating yourself.

What is Your Life's Reflection?

The following assessment was created to help you learn about your life. Answer these questions honestly with the intention of getting some understanding about areas that are ripe for growth. Use your journal to detail your responses.

Mom-Me Assessment

Consider the following:

Financial

1. What would you like to create financially?
2. What are your financial goals? Do you ever think about creating wealth?
3. What resources do you currently utilize to keep a record of your finances?
4. Do you have an understanding of your business and household expenses?
5. Do you know how to locate your financial information and resources easily?
6. Do you pay your expenses on time?
7. Do you live a life that you can afford?
8. What other questions would you like to ask yourself about your finances?

Work/Career

1. Are you happy with your career/work inside or outside of home?
2. What could make your work life better?
3. What could you do right now to change your work situation?
4. Name three things you are merely tolerating in your work.
5. How can you eliminate these from your life immediately?
6. Does your work allow you to express your true talent?
7. Do you often feel physically and mentally exhausted at the end of your work day? Why?
8. What is missing from your work life?

Legacy

1. Are you living the life you always envisioned?
2. What shifts would you like to make to attain your dream life?
3. How do you want to be remembered as mom, as wife, as yourself?

Hobbies

1. What are your hobbies?
2. When was the last time you spent time on these hobbies?
3. How did you feel while doing this activity?
4. Why don't you have hobbies?
5. Do you feel guilty when having personal fun?

Health

1. When did you last visit your doctor?
2. Why haven't you gone to the doctor?
3. Are you healthy?
4. Do you exercise? How often? Why not?
5. What does your ideal health look like for you?
6. What resources do you have at your disposal to exercise?
7. What type of exercise do you like?
8. What is an easy way for you to exercise?

Relational

1. Write down your five most important relationships.
2. Describe the type of influence these relationships have on you (e.g., supportive, demanding, needy).

3. Do you feel loved?
4. Who understands you best?
5. Do you want to establish meaningful relationships?
6. Are your only friends other moms?
7. Do you have relationships that inspire you?
8. Who is you confidante?

Personal

1. What about my life makes me happy?
2. How do I feel when I am happy?
3. Who am I? (How do you describe yourself to others?)
4. What am I most grateful for in my life?
5. How does this make me feel?
6. What makes me proud in my life?
7. What about this makes me feel good?
8. What do I like about myself?

Answering the questions in this simple assessment gives you some perspective on areas with potential for personal growth. These questions are meant to be guidelines and not a complete list. What questions do you need to ask yourself about these areas of your life? What do you really want?

The purpose of this assignment is to get you used to seeing your life completely instead of in fragments. I believe that personal growth should be reflected in various areas of our lives.

The areas of personal growth are referred to as the **wheel of our lives**. There are eight areas of our lives that require personal growth or attention to live a balanced life. The areas are as follows:

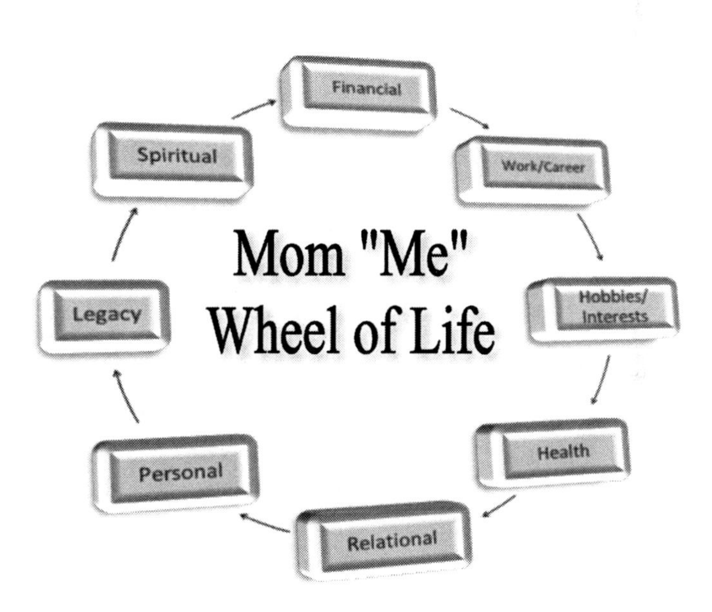

Areas of Balanced Life

Financial	Enhancing the economic security and increasing awareness of the family's financial picture.
Productive Work/Career/ Outlet	Establishing opportunities that allow us to express ourselves productively either in or outside of the home.
Hobbies/ Recreational	Creating meaningful channels to express our passion/s allows us to stay connected to our interests.
Health	Maintaining good physical health by utilizing exercise to energize, relieve stress and reduce anxiety.
Relational	Establishing supportive networks that validate you and provide resources for living life to its fullest.
Personal	Creating opportunities to feel, express, enjoy.
Contribution/ Legacy	Creating a life that has meaning and value, and that allows us to support our family but leaves evidence of living fully.
Spiritual	Creating a means to refuel spiritually by being reflective, prayerful, or engaging in a fellowship of worship.

As we understand ourselves as women, we know we are not single-faceted, instead we are multi-dimensional. When we consider our areas of personal growth, we must also consider the various areas of growth. I believe that to be a whole person you must accomplish several of these developmental areas at the same time. Yes, it is possible to take care of your physical health and grow intellectually and have friendships that you honor. Many times we pick from a small list for ourselves, believing that our world needs to be small in order to manage the demands of home.

Understanding this, I created a definition for the stages of personal growth for mothers. They are the following: **Stagnant, Motion, Acceleration**.

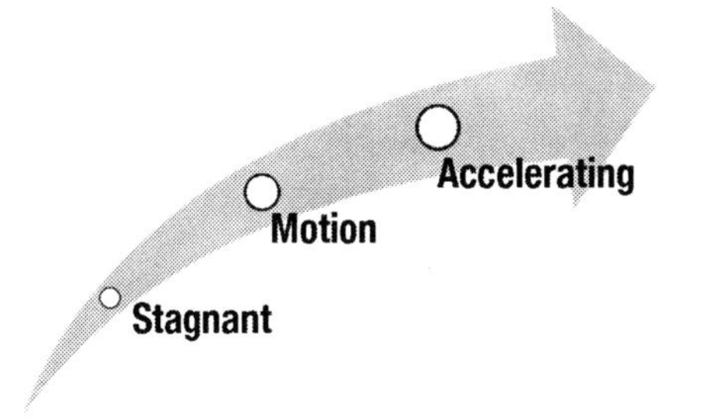

You may look at the Mom "Me" wheel and determine that you are only accomplishing in one of these areas, or you may notice that you have consistently maintained your relationship with friends and family but at the expense of your health. Still, there are several other areas that await you. Take your time, but make the decision to cultivate growth in each of these eight areas.

The first stage of personal growth is STAGNANT

Stagnant means that any growing that happens is void of real change. When you are stagnant in your personal growth you are continuing to do, wear, and look and feel the same every day. This stage is easy because life is comfortable and familiar.

Moms who are stagnant may do any of the following:

- Wear the same clothes multiple times of the week
- Fail to fix their hair in the morning
- Not exercise
- Eat unhealthy foods
- Feel sadness but not know why
- Lack energy
- Lack emotion
- Feel irritable

The reason moms feel this way is because each day presents the same mundane routine. These moms may work outside or inside of the home and still feel like a hamster on a wheel. They feel their lives moving but going nowhere. Admittedly, this is a hard stage to change.

The strategies necessary to change this stage are:

1. **Identify possible areas of growth**. Circle the areas on the personal growth wheel that you would like to improve in your life.

   Financial
   Work/Career
   Hobbies/Recreational
   Health
   Relational
   Personal
   Legacy
   Spiritual

2. **Ask yourself the following questions**
   (a) What shifts can I make in this area of my life?
   (b) What is missing in this area of my life?
   (c) What would I like to see in this area?
   (d) What ability do I have right now to create this change?

3. **Map your behavior as you change**
   (a) Practice makes perfect. Start slowly and begin with one area.
   (b) Allow for transition. Initially you will feel awkward working on this area of your life, because it is unfamiliar. Be patient with your-

self. Give yourself time to feel positive about this new change.

(c) Reward yourself and feel good about making strides. Examples of rewards include the following: get a pedicure/manicure, plan a date with your favorite book in the park, take a walk in a scenic location, or give yourself a facial. Now what reward will you choose?

(d) Repeat this step until it becomes a habit. *Mastering it is the goal.*

4. **Define your values.** Do you know what you value? Do you value rest and clarity of thought? Do you value creativity and expression? As you identify the areas that you want to change, utilizing your value system, make sure your growth objectives resonate with your inner desires.

Sample Values Chart

Respect	Faith	Caring	Relationship	Health
Love	Forgiveness	Spirituality	Pleasure	Discover
Intensity	Adventure	Clarity	Balance	Joy
Learning	Fun	Gratitude	Wellness	Financial Security
Kindness	Persistency	Accountability	Honesty	
Acceptance	Harmony	Fun	Service	Passion
Compassion	Beauty	Creativity	Learning	
*Beauty	Order	Organization	Excited	Competent
Dependable	Respectful	Intelligent		

5. **Develop a realistic plan of what it will take to accomplish these things**. Ask yourself, "What will it take for me to accomplish this task?" Many times we think that the task is bigger than it is. Moms need to break down any plan into bite-size pieces.

   Follow these steps to break down goals.
   They are:
   1. Ask yourself, "What steps do I have to take to get the task accomplished?"
   2. Assign a time to complete each task.(i.e., January 30, 20)
   3. Consider what resources you might need to accomplish this task. (e.g., time, money, baby-sitter, mother's helper, etc.)
   4. Establish checkpoint goals along the way. What do you plan to have accomplished within 15 days, 30 days or 35 days of the actual goal.

6. **Choose two strategies to change at the same time**. Select two areas from your personal growth list to work on together. Many times we will attempt to achieve one area and leave the others because we are accomplishing something. It is imperative that you accomplish your goals in groups. When you create the space and time to complete your objectives, do all that you can in those moments.

7. **Get a buddy to run with**. If possible, find a friend who wants to achieve her own goals. Call one another weekly about your goals. Check in, weigh in and share what is working and what is not working.

8. **Get started!** Don't wait until Monday or until you get the right running shoes. Moms must act now. Things change so quickly in the life of mothers that if you don't act today, you won't start.

9. **Don't check results**. The point in this phase is to begin to identify some areas to improve the inner workings of your life. This does not mean that overnight things are going to be perfect. It does mean that you can immediately begin to move in your life in ways that fulfil you instead of maintaining a life that is unfulfilling.

The second stage of personal growth is MOTION

If you are in motion, you realize some of the areas of personal growth but have not developed a consistent habit of achieving your goals. For example, you may play golf during the spring and summer but fail to add to the list during the winter and fall. The idea is that we understand that we want to continue the activities, events and energy that fuel us. As moms, our work is demanding and we need to release our tension with things that make us laugh, stimulate the mind and make us happy.

Understand there are eight areas of personal growth. When we are in motion we are usually accomplishing up to four areas of personal growth. Using the wheel analogy, we are then able to move but it is still a bumpy ride because there are other parts of ourselves we are not acknowledging.

It is my goal to see every mother have the active ability to create a world that includes her. My friends have always been amazed by my ability to pursue my intellectual and spiritual growth while maintaining hobbies and special interests and pursuing good physical health. I am the perfect coach for you, because I know what it takes to make the time.

The strategies for Motion

1. Date yourself in advance. Plan a date in the future with yourself. Purchase tickets, make reservations or reserve the date with a friend to motivate you toward your goal. New mom tip: Whenever I have a child, I always plan a short date with myself. This might include going to the coffee shop to enjoy a

warm drink, making a visit to the bookstore to read a magazine or enjoying a movie. You decide.

2. Put your self-commitments on a personal calendar. When you make the commitment to yourself, make it official on your family's calendar as well as your personal calendar.

3. Get an accountability partner. This could be a person with her own goals to accomplish or just a favorite friend who is pulling for you.

The last stage of personal growth is ACCELERATION

Acceleration permits moms to soar. When we accelerate, we are able to move forward with our dreams. Generally, we are able to accelerate on that wheel of life as mothers. If you are in a car with square wheels, how fast will you get to your destination? Not very fast. Well, the same is true when we only cultivate two or four areas of our lives as mothers. At a minimum, it is of great benefit to accomplish six to eight areas of our lives. This allows us to have a smoother ride of life. The reason is simple; because we are connecting to and acknowledging ourselves, our love and our interests; we want to move forward with our dreams, plans and goals.

Moms are under pressure to produce happy and successful children. The truth of the matter is that in order for us to create these wonderful children we must be willing to commit hours to helping our children study, practice, understand and flourish. This often leaves us with little for ourselves.

I have found if you want to ensure that you take care of your interests each day, you have to place them at the top of the list. This may sound selfish. However, I am not saying to stop meeting the needs of your children. I am suggesting that if you don't put yourself first, then you will never accomplish anything for yourself. The night before, plan the things you want to accomplish for yourself. Next, tell all necessary parties what you need from them. Sometimes you will need your husband to help you in order to accomplish the task. Being clear about what you want to do, will allow you to solicit the help of others.

Your goal is personal growth. Living a life void of growth is neither rich nor healthy. We want to be positive examples of success to our children, and we can't be if we're living a life that does not reflect our hearts. A life that is rich with personal growth reflects the desires of our hearts.

"A mother's happiness is like a beacon, lighting up the future but reflected also on the past in the guise of fond memories"
– Honoré de Balzac

The Strategies for Acceleration are:

1. Continue to add to your list from the mom-Me wheel. Be creative.

2. Ask yourself the following questions: What are my personal visions, missions and passions? What are my goals?

3. Create an affirmation or self-talk statement that affirms you. (i.e., I love how much energy I have when I exercise therefore, I will work-out 3 times a week)

The challenge for you is to take a good look at the life you have created and examine it thoroughly. Is this the life you have planned, or is this the life that you have gotten by default? Making the decision to guide your life is the best way to ensure personal growth and success.

You must obtain a "PH.D." in me.
"PH.D." stands for Personal Healing Done.
A PH.D. is a must for all moms.
Earn a PH.D in mom-Me!

The five top reasons to personally grow

1. You deserve it! Take some time and write down why you deserve to be your best. What do you give your family?

2. Your children are watching your example of success! Do your children see a balance in your life? Do your children learn to be appreciative from watching you? What has your life taught your children about personal space?

3. You want a better life! Know that life is offering you more. You have gotten in the way of a life that you can enjoy. You want to be happy.

4. Why not be happy! Live a life that is satisfying.

5. Personal growth will allow you to connect with yourself and figure out who you are! Taking the time to get to know yourself will allow you to change the course of your life. I have clients who have accepted the demands of life believing that they are forever going to be unfulfilled, unexcited and unhappy. Why accept this as your reality when you can choose your life?

Chapter Objective

- To identify specific areas for personal growth.

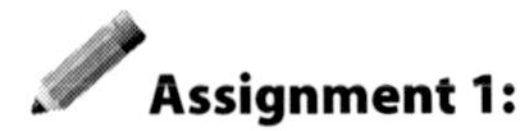

Assignment 1:

Look at your life as it is and consider improving other areas on the wheel of life to enhance balance and wholeness.

1. Identify two areas in which you would like to personally grow.

2. What action can you take today to begin to realize growth in this area? (e.g., if the area is health: go to the gym or walk with your child for a minimum of 30 minutes three times a week or schedule doctor visits.)

3. Over the next 30 days, what steps can you take to make your growth a priority?

4. What does your goal require to make it happen?

Assignment 2:

Look at the wheel of life. Identify two areas that you would like to change today. Answer the following questions about those areas:

1. What do I want to accomplish in this area of my life?

2. What resources or requirements does this activity require to make it happen?

3. What are the possibilities once I make this change?

4. What are the benefits to me? My family?

Practices:

✓ Email our mom-Me success partner daily, weekly or bi-weekly, depending on what you have decided, on the action that you have taken toward your goal.

✓ Take a minimum of 15 minutes each day to plan how you will accomplish your objective the next day.

Share your results at www.timeformom-me.com on our community forum. Once you've completed the assignments and practices, download and print your PHD certificate at www.timeformom-me.com/forms.

CHAPTER 3

Finding Time

Melissa works 60 hours a week. She awakens at 6am and works until 6pm. She struggles with finding personal time to go to the gym, to run personal errands, and to pursue a personal passion. She has a nanny, but finds her days are often occupied with meetings, appointments, unplanned interruptions and schedules. She longs for more flexibility.

Linda, home-schooler and mother of four, works both day and night. She wakes up at 5:30am to prepare for the day. She teaches the children, coordinates all their extra-curricular activities, and manages the household responsibilities. She works until 9:30pm every day. She can't even go to the bathroom without being disturbed.

The purpose of this chapter is to help mothers find time for themselves. As a busy mother myself, I understand the specific strategies that moms must employ to succeed. Unlike most time-management or organize-your-life self-help books, I will provide you with specific techniques created just for mothers.

As moms, we have distinct challenges that consistently prevent us from finding personal time. Some of the challenges are self-inflicted, such as mommy guilt, fatigue, lack of know-how and supermom attitudes, while others are external, such as unscheduled interruptions, changes in plans and the family schedule. This chapter will shed some light on all of these challenges that are presented in the life of a mother.

"If evolution really works, how come
mothers only have two hands"
– Milton Berle

In previous chapters we have discussed your blueprint of motherhood, the benefits of personal growth solutions. Now that you are clear about your blueprint; have identified areas for personal growth, the next phase is finding time to self-accomplish.

A mom's day is hectic. No two days are exactly the same. Although we may have the same events in our day, we are never quite sure what the day will hold. In the midst of a home or work project, you could get a call from the school nurse telling you to pick up your child from school. While attempting to read a magazine, you might get interrupted 10 times.

Symptoms of Unbalanced Life

Answer these questions honestly with the intention of getting some understanding about areas you want to change. Use a journal to detail your responses.

Mom-Me Assessment

Consider the following:

1. Overscheduled. Do you run from one event/activity to another?
2. Overcommitted: Are you signing up for a host of activities because a good mom should do these commitments?

3. Are you reactive? Are you always putting out the wildfires in your life?
4. Do you feel there are never enough hours in a day?
5. Does your life lack planning?
6. Are your family activities driven by the words should and ought to?
7. Do you struggle with relaxation?
8. Do you feel you are the only person capable of doing a good job at __________?
9. Do you define yourself by doing for others?
10. Do you have trouble saying "No"?
11. Do you often find yourself doing things that you don't want to do?

If you have answered yes to four or fewer, then you are able to strike a balance in your life. If you have answered yes to between five and eight, then you are in need of a balance makeover. Over eight, then you are out of balance.

Steps To Creating More Balance

1. Acknowledge that you are out of balance (e.g., I am out of balance).

2. Ask yourself the following, "What is making me feel out of balance?" (e.g., I know that I am out of balance, because I work all the time and have very little time to enjoy life.)

3. What does balance look like to you? (e.g., balance means that I can stop every day to simply enjoy a nice cup of tea.)

4. What resources do you have to help you manage balance in your life? (e.g., well, I can take 10minutes to sit still and have a cup of tea.)

5. Which of these resources can you take ownership of today? (e.g., I can make a commitment to do this at least once a day as soon as I get home from work.)

6. What is possible if you utilize this change? (e.g., it's possible that I will feel more relaxed as I greet my family instead of grumpy, snappy and irritated)

7. Is this a change you would like to make? Yes? Why?

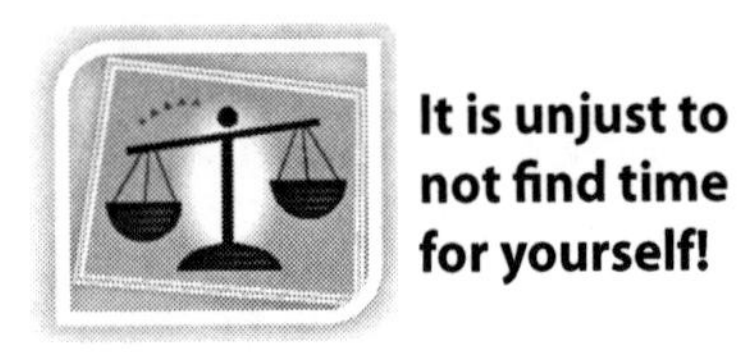

A Mother's Work Is Never Done

As moms, we have a terrific opportunity to share in the joys, triumphs and wonders of our children. If you are like most moms you have found a way to be an active part of your children's world. Helping them to engage, explore and master the world around them requires discipline, commitment and love.

As you tend to the needs of your family, you must find ways to meet your own needs. Have you ever considered doing something for yourself while doing something for your family? At this moment, I want you to dream about your ideal day. What would you be doing? Who would be there? How long would it last?

What if I told you that you can create that dream life by making a few simple changes in your life? Would you believe me?

Too often as moms we believe that our lives await us after the children are older, go to bed or graduate from school. What if I told you it is possible to enjoy your life today by simply taking a few small steps?

Reflect on each of the following questions. Use your journal section to answer.

Mom-Me Assessment

Consider the following:

1. What about my life makes me feel good?
2. How would people describe me?
3. What are my greatest accomplishments to date?
4. How much of the day do I spend doing things to make myself happy?

5. What do I do for myself each day?
6. If I spent time doing only things that make me happy, what would I be doing?
7. If I only spent time with people who made me happy, who would that be?
8. How much fun do I want in my life?
9. What do I like to do in order to be happy?

Now that you have answered the questions above, you have an understanding of how out of balance you are and what your ideal life would look like. Now, look specifically at your actual days to create a plan to help you find time to do what you love.

Moms: What are you doing all day?

Mothers have tons of activities that go on the list of Contribution Activities. Contribution activities are activities that have to be accomplished for the family but don't necessarily leave a record of their successful completion. These are the catch-all activities that go along with motherhood, including:

Contribution Activities

Nursing	Tending to flu/ colds	Bathing children
Mealtime Planning and Preparation	Laundry	Housework
Carpool	Running errands	Checking Homework
Organizing	Supervising Play	Playing

Assignment 1:

Write down some of your most common Contribution Activities. They might include: reading a story, taking the necessary visit to the playground, important searches for rocks or leaves, spending time in the observation area for an extracurricular activity, etc. You name it. We all have them. Feel free to duplicate any of the activities above. Write them below or use your journal.

My Contributions

1. ______________________________

2. _______________ _______________

3. _______________ _______________

4. _______________ _______________

5. _______________ _______________

6. _______________ _______________

You get the idea! Now, ask yourself what you can do for yourself while accomplishing these same contribution activities. This might mean that you will share your love of classical literature with your children during story time, or that you will encourage the children to take a short hike while looking for rocks so that you can exercise. I call this blending.

What is blending?

You want to exercise.

Your child wants to play on the playground.

While she plays, you do squats or jump rope!

Blending is when moms combine their personal objectives with a family activity in order to self-accomplish. What I am suggesting is that we look for ways to blend ourselves into our lives.

Other examples include:

- While preparing the baths in the evening, play soft music you enjoy.

- At the playground, consider creative ways to exercise at the playground while playing with your children. Consider chasing the children at a game of tag or taking your own adventure on the swing.

- During carpool, pack a bag for you that contains your favorite healthy snack, book, calendar or crossword puzzles.

- At the birthday party, make a friend for you. It is possible to still make personal connections with others.

- At home, assign a time for everyone to D.E.A.R. (Drop Everything And Read). This will give you some time to finish that book you started.

The idea is to create opportunities to self-accomplish during the activities that we naturally do as moms.

Most moms have done the exact opposites. We don't seize the opportunities to do anything for ourselves until the day has ended. Many of us are still searching for that extra time at the end of the day, week or years to do something for ourselves.

"Now, as always, the most automated appliance in the household is the mother"
– Beverly Jones

Taking this time to create a list of blending possibilities will allow you to be playful and responsive to your needs. Bring yourself into the activities with your children. With some of these activities it's tougher than others. But it is possible for all of these activities to provide some level of support for us as we support and nurture our little ones.

How to Blend

When blending, ask yourself the following questions:

1. What goal/s would I like to accomplish? Do you have weight-loss goals, friendships to establish, hobbies, or a specific interest like hiking, golfing, cooking, etc.?

2. Identify the amount of time and space necessary to achieve this objective. Does this goal have to be accomplished all at once, or is it possible to break it into bite-size portions?

3. Identify a place in your day where you can implement this objective. Is it possible to park four blocks away from school and walk to pick up the children? Could you read that book during the soccer practice?

Examples of a Blended Life

On the way from home from my children's playgroup, they always fall asleep. Instead of going straight home I go to my favorite neighborhood park where I can see the lake. I drive up close to the lake and I open my sunroof, play the soft music I love and read my favorite magazine. For that hour I am transported, renewed and rested.

– Stephanie, mother of three children between two and ten

At track practice for my daughter, I started to train with the team. I used to complain that I didn't have time to exercise. These days, I find myself at practice 3 times a week. This presented the perfect opportunity to support my daughter and to exercise for me. Now I am able to run three miles without stopping.

– Allison, mother of a 13-year-old daughter

In the morning when I make breakfast for the children; I light a candle for me. I love the smell of aromatic candles. Now while I do something that I have to do in the morning to prepare for the day, I do something that transcends my environment.

– Shawn, mother of two children between one and six

Blending Opportunities

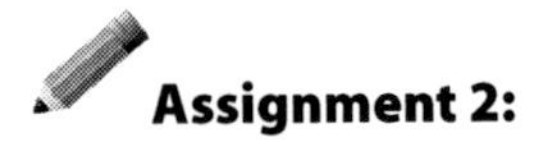

Assignment 2:

Write down what you can do for yourself for each of the activities that you identified from assignment 1. (Copy your contribution activities from assignment 1) Be creative. At first it might take you a minute because you never thought about doing any self-accomplishing task while supporting your children.

Be patient with yourself and give yourself time to Dream Big.

	My Contributions	My Blending
1.	____________________	____________________
2.	____________________	____________________
3.	____________________	____________________
4.	____________________	____________________
5.	____________________	____________________
6.	____________________	____________________

Now commit to self-accomplishing! How many possibilities daily do you REALLY have in your busy schedule to include you?

Practices:

Take a snapshot of your typical day, and look for the possibilities to self-accomplish each day. Everyday identify a minimum of one activity where you can do something for both your family and yourself.

Use the following chart to write down your family's daily schedule. Each week, update your schedule for the week to include any new activities. The purpose of this calendar activity is to make you aware of all you do. Don't be shy here. I want you to include everything you do to make your days happen.

Too often we minimize the small activities such as making dinner, washing laundry, grocery shopping. This exercise will start by running the span of your week. Take some time and really think about how you spend your days. The purpose of the exercise is to help you see how you spend your days. Let's begin:

Under "Activity," indicate how you spend your time with your family. Include any and all activities that you perform for your family daily, including making breakfast, volunteering at school, work commitments, extra-curricular activities, dinner preparation/clean-up, bath , story-time, night-time clean-up, and so forth.

In addition, look at the time of day each of these activities is performed. Be specific.

Next, where are you performing these activities? In your car, at home, at work, at the playground, or some other location?

Finally, list any possibility for you to do something for you with each activity.

Visit www.timeformom-me.com/forms for a printable version of this chart to accurately capture the activities for each week.

Snapshot of your day

Monday

Activity	Time	Location	Blending Activity
i.e. Soccer Practice	*5:30–6:30pm*	*Soccer Field*	*Read a book in the car.*

Tuesday

Activity	Time	Location	Blending Activity

Wednesday

Activity	Time	Location	Blending Activity

Thursday

Activity	Time	Location	Blending Activity

Friday

Activity	Time	Location	Blending Activity

Saturday

Activity	Time	Location	Blending Activity

Sunday

Activity	Time	Location	Blending Activity

Promise yourself today you will incorporate "YOU" into your life.

Opportunities to incorporate ourselves into our own lives are all around us. For a mom to self-accomplish, she needs to know what we are attempting to create. Taking this time to create different lists of blending possibilities will allow you to be "planful" and responsive to your needs.

Too often, I hear stories of moms who go days, weeks, months and years putting themselves on hold. These mothers are looking for permission and the opportunity to enjoy their lives. Creating a list of possibilities for you makes it easier to find small ways to realize personal happiness every day.

The Benefits of Blending Your Life

✓ Blending creates opportunities to enjoy your life daily.

✓ Blending is an efficient use of time.

✓ Blending gives moms a new perspective when planning their days.

✓ Blending allows children to see self-care in action.

✓ Blending helps mothers find easy ways to incorporate themselves into their own lives every day.

✓ Blending allows mothers to consciously acknowledge their needs and wants daily without putting themselves on hold.

✓ Blending gives mothers new options. It provides a new mindset for self-care.

Additional strategies on blending

1. Make the things you enjoy easily accessible. Make your car your mobile university. Take your books on CD or MP3 with you for your vehicle. Pack a book/magazine for you.

2. Play when your children play. So often we tend to work when our children play. Try to play when they play. While your children play in the backyard, read a book for you, jump rope for you, or journal. As moms, many times we keep every second of our day busy when we could look for opportunities to enjoy what is before us.

3. Make your environment reflect the things that you love such as, beautiful flowers, candles, or gardens.

Visit www.timeformom-me.com/forms for a free list of my 20 favorite ways to blend your life. I want to hear your blending strategies too. Share at www.timeformom-me.com.

Affirmation

I took an action for me today and it felt great!

____

(Your Signature)

CHAPTER 4

Finding Meaning

Redefining and Creating Change in Your Life

Here are two examples of typical moms: *She is a corporate executive who has realized a lot of professional success. She is known as a hard worker and is a top performer. She also has a family, consisting of three children and has been married for seven years. She had a dream of becoming a caterer, a dream she felt was impossible. She felt that the demands of home and work would never allow her to do what she really wanted to do. Every year she talked about her love for catering with her family and friends. Everyone thought it was impossible because she worked 50+ hours a week in her career. So she decided to put her dreams on the shelf.*

Another is a stay-at-home mom and a very dedicated mom to her three children. She has managed to meet the needs of her children effortlessly. She has enrolled her children in piano, tae kwon do, t-ball and gymnastics. As a wife she is equally committed. She manages to have dinner ready most days when her husband returns from work. She is considerate of him and makes sure that she and the children give her husband space and time to relax in the comfort of his home. She is always busy. She continues this way every day.

This is only half of the story...what is missing?

What is missing from your life?
What do you want for you?
Do you still have dreams left to accomplish?
What are they?

A Mother's Work

Why is it that, as women and as moms, we believe we have to sacrifice ourselves to be wonderful contributors?

You've been on the plane before take off--the flight attendant instructs what to do in the event of an emergency. We are instructed to put on our air mask FIRST, before helping others. As moms we should employ the basic life saving strategies of the airlines.

Let's talk about why this is important.

In order to truly help someone else you must begin by helping yourself. In order to truly be a wonderful contributor, you must help yourself FIRST.

Imagine that you are a cup that is always half-full or empty. Your cup is never full because you don't allow yourself the opportunity to replenish and renew. How can you then fill another cup?

When we give from a full cup we are kinder, nicer, more patient, more creative and loving. Helping yourself first enables you to better help others.

Remember your mommy script? Well, your children are watching your example of self-care and neglect. We would never tell our children to give their lunch away and go hungry or to give their friends all of their best pencils and leave themselves with nothing. Yet, we teach our children indirectly every day that we are not important.

Quite frankly, you deserve to do something for yourself because you give so much to the lives of your family. As a mom coach, I encourage my clients to create a supportive network of friends and family, establish a work/life balance, and set personal boundaries.

Before I tell you how to "fill your cup," take a few moments to define your life in general. Find a quiet location, free of interruptions. Use your journal to detail your responses. It is important to be as open and honest with yourself while completing this exercise. Utilize these questions as a guide to get you to think about what your life means. There are no right or wrong answers, just insight on the areas that requiring more care.

Mom-Me Assessment

Consider the following:

1. What about my life makes me feel good?
2. How would people describe me?
3. What are my greatest accomplishments to date?

4. How much time of the day do I spend doing things to make myself happy?

5. What do I do for myself each day?

6. If I spent time doing only things that make me happy, what would I be doing?

7. If I only spent time with people that made me happy, who would that be?

8. How much fun do I want in my life?

9. What do I like to do to be happy?

10. Do I feel guilty when doing something for myself?

11. Yes No Why?

12. When did I last experience this guilty feeling? Describe the situation.

13. (Using the example from #11) What steps could I take to minimize my feelings of guilt?

Most women allow the emotions of guilt and shame to influence their life choices. We feel guilty about the things we have already accomplished and also for the things we have yet to accomplish.

Have you ever made plans to go out with a friend when, just before leaving, one of your children started to cry hysterically? You immediately thought maybe I should not go out now, because my child needs me. If you chose to go out anyway, I guarantee that you called home once or twice to make sure matters had not gotten worse, and you probably still felt guilty for leaving in the first place.

"She never quite leaves her children at home,
even when she doesn't take them along"
– Margaret Culkin Banning

Or, maybe whenever you think of doing something for yourself you simply feel selfish. Maybe you are thinking that it is unfair for you to put any of your needs on the family's agenda.

As mothers, there are several things that keep us away from our dreams, plans and goals. Any time you want to make a change you must raise your standards.

In order to assign meaning and value to your life, you must:

✓ Define a clear vision for your life.

✓ Eliminate self-defeating habits that stop you in your tracks.

✓ Identify triggers that keep you from accomplishing your goals.

Defining a Clear Vision for Your Life

What do you want for you? Consider where you are right now and think about where you want to be.

Maybe you want to pursue excellence in your physical health, or perhaps you want to be well traveled. Once you identify what you want, you can begin to make small changes or adjustments toward this vision.

What are your dreams? A dream is your personal ambition. The compositions of our dreams have many forms. The first are our mental images.

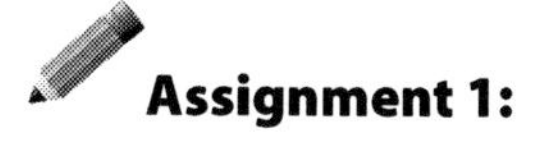

Assignment 1:

Take a few moments to journal your responses. Read the following questions below. Close your eyes, and reflect before you respond.

1. What do you really want for your life?

2. What comes to your mind?

3. Are you envisioning peace and harmony, recreation, or that career you've always wanted?

4. What do you see for you?

5. How do these images make you feel? Relaxed, happy, anxious, or excited?

This is a great exercise to start figuring out what you want for your life.

Perhaps you want to lose those extra pounds from pregnancy, or maybe you want to enroll in school for some graduate courses. Everything starts with a vision for your life. For example, once you decide that your personal health is a priority, you can then set the goal to lose 15 pounds. Next, you will take the necessary steps to achieve that objective by locating a local gym, by working out, or by identifying a person in your community to walk or run with four times each week. It's that simple.

Ask yourself how you are going to accomplish your goal. The most important question to ask is what you plan to accomplish. Being clear on what to accomplish is the key to our success.

Changing our life takes commitment. It means that we have to overcome our fears, excuses, procrastination and our schedule to create the life we want. Many times we have to change the way we think and the way we behave to clear the way for the things we want.

Eliminating Self-Defeating Habits

Make a commitment with yourself that once you identify a vision for your life, you will become a partner with yourself in the process of change. We have to be our own instruments for change. We have to create the change we want by reinventing our behaviors. Bad habits keep us stuck in our old ways. We need to make different choices that aid our process to self-accomplishment.

Reasons We Stop What We Start

- Assuming we already know the outcome of a new experience. Have you done this? You want to try something new and different but you presume to know what the new experience will bring.

- Labeling ourselves by saying things like "I'm not good at…"

- Over-generalizing any new experience to suggest that it is not good. For example, maybe you arranged a night out with some friends for the first time. Upon returning home you described the evening as a waste of time and said that the restaurant food lacked the quality of home.

- Blaming others for what we have not done for ourselves

- Comparing ourselves to others. When we do this we always compare our weaknesses to the strengths of others.

The idea here is to begin to make conscious choices. Think about what you want to accomplish, and choose to honor your desires with action every day. Identify and remove thoughts from your mind that defeat you. If we want to change our lives, we must change our old self-defeating patterns. We must begin by believing we deserve that which we desire. Many times we don't believe we deserve the very thing we are trying to accomplish.

Align yourself with the possibility of success!

Identifying the triggers that keep you from accomplishing your goals

A series of events could change at any moment when we try to self-accomplish. In an instant, our children could become ill, skin their knees, or engage in a battle of sibling rivalry. The workload could seem impossible. To self-accomplish, you need to be proactive. Account for as many of these looming unscheduled interruptions. For example, have you ever attempted to read a book and yet never managed to read even one page? What happened? Asking yourself this important question can help you anticipate what your most common distractions are so that you can plan for them.

Triggers are simply distractions. You may find that whenever you are loading the dishwasher after dinner and attempting to listen to an audio book, your children begin to disagree and argue, preventing you from hearing your audio selection.

Recognizing common distractions is important, because it clarifies what you need to change in your day to self-accomplish. Ask yourself: "How can I overcome this obstacle, situation or distraction?" If the children fight when you unload the dishwasher, why not propose a time to Drop Everything And Read – DEAR – for the children after dinner? This will allow you to complete part of your audio book and give the children a task to accomplish.

Kelly's daughter, Stacy, always wanted her mom whenever Kelly attempted to read a book. I taught Kelly this simple technique called mirroring with her 18 month old. Instead of sneaking away to read, Kelly made reading a two-person activity, one she explained to Stacy. "We're going to read for 15 minutes. This is my book. Go get your Elmo book so you can read, too."

Stacy got her Elmo book and sat down next to Kelly. After a few minutes, Stacy put her book down and climbed into her mother's lap.

"No, not yet," Kelly said. "Reading time isn't over. You can get another book if you like, but we're going to read some more."

Stacy got another book. The first time Kelly tried the technique, she had to keep sending Stacy back for books; but, after a while, Stacy caught on.

Assignment 2: Complete the distraction log.

When do I most often have distractions? What am I doing? How long do they last?

Right now, I want you to write down 10 ways that you become distracted at home. Consider different times of the days and during different kinds of activities.

Activity *(What are you doing?)*	**Distraction** *(What is the distraction?)*	**Time of the Day** *(Breakfast, Dinner, cleaning, etc.)*
1.		
2.		
3.		
4.		
5.		
6.		
7.		
8.		
9.		
10.		

Mirroring Steps

- Talk with your children and tell them the activity that you plan to accomplish and the amount of time it will take. *Mom is going to write in her diary for 15 minutes.*

- Have your child mirror your activity. Teach your young children initially in one-, three- and five-minute intervals until they understand this activity. *Stacy is going to write on her pad for 15 minutes.*

- Remember to be patient and loving but consistent while reinforcing your child. *It is still writing time; so, here is Stacy's crayon and paper.*

Reward your child when you are finished.

As moms, we have to be proactive to include ourselves into our days. Taking the time to list your most common distractions will assist you in finding reasonable ways to self-accomplish in the company of your children.

Now you understand what you need to do to create the mindset for change in your life. Change requires us to redefine our priorities.

Remember the moms that were mentioned earlier. Well, the corporate executive learned that if she wanted to have a catering business she could. She began to schedule herself into her life a few hours a week. She accomplished something for her business every week. She went from believing that she had no time to plan events to planning three events. The largest event was a wedding with more than 200 guests.

The mom learned to set some personal boundaries with her children. She put her children to bed at 8:00 pm, understanding that this gave her some down time after a day of giving. In addition, she asked her husband if he would support her taking some time to take piano lessons. She can now read music and play the piano.

Both of these moms used the techniques taught in this book to accomplish their once impossible goals. It's all about clarifying the changes you want in your life. It is possible, and your family loves you and will accommodate your wishes. Just ask!

Strategies for developing a clear vision for your life and redefining your dream

1. Develop a clear vision for your life and redefine your dream.

2. Look at where you are and where you want to go next. Then begin to make small adjustments to propel you toward your goal. Stay committed to what you want by listening to this book and by reviewing your journal.

3. Remember to eliminate self-defeating habits. If you want a different outcome, then do something differ-

ent. Don't expect to achieve a different result if you continue to do the same things.

4. Identify the triggers preventing moms from achieving their objectives. Become the expert of your life. Figure out what the reoccurring interruptions are that get you off track. Be proactive and solution-oriented.

5. The goal is to create a life you love.

6. Increase your standards for living.

7. Dream big for your life. You deserve it. Create a life that is rich with personal fulfilment and self-connection.

8. Change unhelpful belief patterns. Get rid of thoughts that say you cannot take care of yourself and still be a good mother. These are untrue. Instead, look for ways to:

    ✓ Develop new strategies for change.

    ✓ Create a new way to live that reflects your values.

    ✓ Create your dreams, plans and goals by applying my strategies to make the changes that will help redefine your life.

You can have the life you want. Remember that self-care is not negotiable, but necessary to be the best parent possible. Yes, you can!

Practices:

Identify your goals. Expand your list of goals from your exercise in the personal growth chapter. Look at more areas of your life that you want to change, (e.g., physical, social, intellectual, financial, spiritual). Identify two/three goals for each of these areas. Make your goals Believable, Achievable, and Time Measurable. Goals should be clearly and simply stated. For example, I will eat healthy food at each meal of the day. When establishing goals, be specific and assign a time that identifies when you achieve this goal. Most importantly, commit to your goals. Mark your calendar every day you have worked toward your goal.

Affirmation

I took an action for me today and it felt great!

____

(Your Signature)

Moms are always looking for great recipes to make the perfect meal. Here is the recipe for enhancing your life esteem or assigning your life meaning.

Ingredients:

courage
big dreams
goals
commitment
solutions

Preparation:

1. Set your temperature to the highest setting. In other words, have an open mind and heart.
2. Look at where you are and where you want to go next. Then, begin to make small adjustments to propel you toward your purpose.
3. Stay committed. To avoid losing focus, state your goals every day. Journaling your feelings and progress always helps.
4. Watch out for self defeating habits. If you want a different outcome, then do something differently.
5. Be aware of the triggers that keep you from achieving your objectives. Be proactive about finding solutions to the distractions that get you off track.

Yield:

A healthy serving of a life you love!

If you love this recipe, share your versions on our community forum at www.timeformom-me.com.

CHAPTER 5

Finding Connection

Moms, What is Your Life Teaching You?

Pretend your life is a mirror. Your life is a mirror of your emotional and social health, your physical strength or weakness, your interests and favorite pastimes. What does your personal mirror reflect?

Answer the following questions to help you see your reflection. Use your journal to detail your responses:

Mom-Me Assessment

Consider the following:

1. Who are your closest friends? When did you last spend three hours or more with these friends?

2. What are your hobbies? How much time have you spent doing these?

3. When was the last time you saw a play or concert for you?

4. Do you like your wardrobe? What looks good on you?

5. How do you relax? What do you enjoy doing at home?

6. Do you like your body? What is your favorite physical trait? Which traits would you like to change?

7. Are you happy? What is the evidence of your happiness?

8. What do you like about yourself? What makes you special?
9. Name one item in your home that is just for you. How often do you get to enjoy this item?
10. What do you love about your life? When do you experience this?
11. What must you change about your life?
12. Are you getting enough rest? What time do you go to bed? What time do you wake each day?
13. How is your diet?
14. What other questions do you need to ask yourself?

When you see yourself in your life mirror, do you see the life you envisioned? As moms, we forget to think about our lives while we create the lives of our children. Remember although it is a wonderful experience to create memories, plans and dreams for your children, it is your life too.

"What price we pay for the glory of motherhood"
– Isadora Duncan

Mothering is a process of giving, loving and celebrating. It has its heart-breaks and disappointments as well. Choosing to be mothers who celebrate the roles and responsibilities of motherhood, we must, at the same time, realize that mothering is not enough to complete us.

Motherhood does not completely define us but enhances what already is. For example, if you are healthy, then you have the opportunity to share that piece of you with your family. If you have a supportive network of friends and family, then you are able to teach your children the benefits of being loved by a world that is bigger than you. This teaches your children the benefits of trusting and sharing themselves with others.

Trish, a mother of two children between the ages of three and eight, was too tired to encourage her children to go to after school activities. She vowed to get more energy. She made the decision to connect through exercise each morning before work. She walked at 5:00 am with one other neighbor.

After two months, she formed a neighborhood walking club. Today, Trish is 20lbs lighter and has consistent opportunities to share with friends and exercise.

Now, Trish encourages her children to participate in soccer and basketball activities to promote their own physical fitness.

Whatever your reflection, you will share that with your children. If your reflection is one of frustration, disappointment and regret, guess what? You will share those also. So now is your opportunity to learn to appreciate your reflection of love, respect, admiration, acceptance and nurturing. A reflection is powerful because it shows us who we really are. Who are you really? What defines you?

The reflection questions are provided to help you connect with yourself. Many moms have not taken the time to ask themselves important and relevant questions about how they connect to the essentials of living. Often I speak with mothers who have no sense of connection to themselves. They want to know which questions to ask themselves. Using these powerful questions will help guide you to ask yourself the necessary questions to self-connect.

The Results of the Lack of Connection

✓ Inability to feel
✓ Unable to identify preferences

✓ Confusion about personal choices
✓ Afraid of failure or the unknown
✓ Overly analytical about choices
✓ Feeling overwhelmed about making decisions
✓ Clueless
✓ Insecure

Let's start changing those feelings.

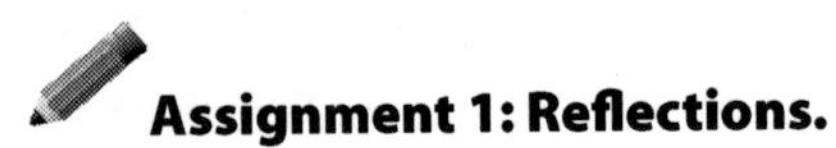

Assignment 1: Reflections.

Write in the space below, or use your journal.

First ask yourself, "What do I like about myself?" Write down what you like about the following:

Physical Features Blank spaces are not allowed. Consider your favorite physical attributes.

List your physical favorites from you best traits to your least favorite.

1. ____

2. ____

3. ____

4. ____

5. ____

Relationships

What type of friend are you? To answer this question, look at your closest friendships. How would you describe your closest friendships? How would your friends describe you as a friend?

List your friendship attributes from your best traits to your least favorite.

1. ____

2. ____

3. ____

4. ____

5. ____

Hobbies

What activities do you enjoy? When answering this question, consider the activities that you currently enjoy. If you are struggling here, then consider the activities that you enjoyed prior to having children.

List your activities from your favorite to the least favorite.

1. ____

2. ____

3. ____

4. ____

5. ____

Finding Time

When was the last time you did something for you? When answering this question, think about how you feel when doing something for yourself. Do you feel guilty, selfish or frivolous when you take time for you?

List the activities that you did for yourself from your favorite to the least favorite.

1. ______________________________

2. ______________________________

3. ______________________________

4. ______________________________

5. ______________________________

Physical appearance

List the last time that you bought an outfit that you loved. Do you know what looks great on you?

Sometimes as moms we say that we are going to wait until we shed unwanted pounds, stop nursing or go back to work before we invest in an outfit that makes us look great. Many times we struggle with the practicality of splurging for ourselves. Is this you?

When was the last time you purchased an outfit you loved? What outfit was it? Where did you get it?

When did you wear it last?

1. ____

2. ____

3. ____

4. ____

5. ____

Now that you have completed this exercise, you have an idea of what your life is reflecting to you.

Your life may be reflecting a greater need for personal space or quiet time. Perhaps your life is reflecting a desire to connect socially with friends or establish meaningful hobbies. The goal of any reflection is learn to love and appreciate what you see. Do you like what you see?

As your coach, I want to help you enhance your view of you. When you look at yourself I want you to love what you see, respect your limits and appreciate your gifts.

Here are five steps to consider looking at your reflection:

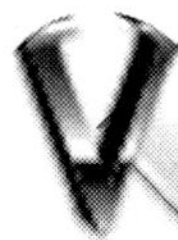

Visualize your best self when looking at your reflection. Visualize yourself as productive, loving and caring. Remove the limiting self-defeating obstacles that keep us stuck and encumbered.

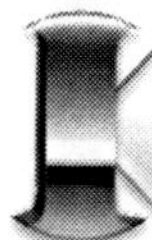

Initiate the change you want. Begin with action! Start today to implement some of your favorites from your reflection list. Use this list over and over to give you a guide of the new things that you want to enhance your life today.

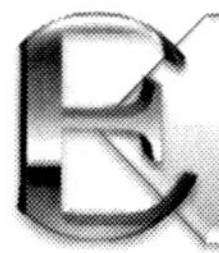

Encourage yourself with words of acceptance and affirmation Use words that make you feel victorious instead of language that leaves you feeling hopeless. Write down positive affirmations about your reflection and post them on a 3 X5 note cards.

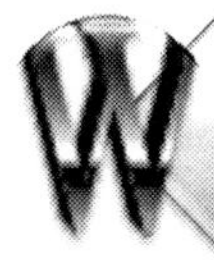

Work the plan. Create a plan of action to enhance your view of you.

Self-Connection

When you take the time to self-connect, you create a space in your life to hear from your inner desires. What are the desires of your heart? What do you really want?

When you spend your days fielding the requests of little people who direct your days, how do you self-connect?

You must employ the following strategies to self-connect as a mother. They are:

1. Assign a space in your home as a **Connection Place**. A connection place is a place where you can go uninterrupted every day. This could be your favorite sofa by the window in your living-room or it could be a vanity that reflects your beauty. A connection place creates a place in your home that fuels you and fills you. This is your home get-away. Most importantly, it is your physical symbol/representation of peace at home.

2. Meet in that connection space a minimum of 15 minutes each day. I believe every mom deserves peace in her life daily. At a minimum, 15 minutes.

3. Equip your space with your tools. Your tools are the following: The Time For mom-Me book, a journal, special music, visual pictures that motivate you toward your goal. Your tools will prove an invaluable resource because by creating these 15 minutes to connect with yourself daily, you will discover who you are. This book will be your best friend as you do the work necessary to redefine who you are.

During the time that you spend in your connection place, you will slowly discover who you are. You will better hear your voice, and you will plan yourself into each day. My goal for you is for you to be present in your life everyday. You will no longer be in a quandary on how to include yourself in every area of your day. You will understand the steps to make this possible and I, your mom coach, will show you how to do it.

You will become a nicer person to your family. You will become better able to love your family because you love yourself. You will become a better nurturer because you will truly have nurtured yourself. Essentially, I am saying that learning who you are will enable you to present your best self to your family.

We have had it all mixed up. We have expected moms to balance the impossible with a smile. The reason I excel as a mother is because I excel as a person. When I am in the company of my children, I am whole, not scattered, fragmented or broken. What about you? What if it were possible to enjoy your life consistently? What if you did not have to have bad days – or days where mommy lost it – because you had a handle on you?

I have been either a stay-at- home-mom (sahm) or a work-at-home-mom (wahm) over the last nine years. During this time I have always consistently found ways to pursue my happiness every day even in the company of my children. This process taught me how to be peaceful, loving, respectful, whole, funny, and spontaneous. All the traits that I first treated myself to showed up in my parenting of my children. I don't have to tell my children do as I say; instead, they know that they have a mom who is present and whole in their lives.

"One good mother is worth a hundred schoolmasters"
– George Herbert

It's All About Self-Connection

When we create a space in our lives to hear from our inner desires, we set the framework for something great. Taking a moment to get quiet every day or every evening will provide us with the time to think and consider new possibilities and opportunities.

What is your something great? What types of connection do you want to see at work in your life?

Defining your life is a commitment that takes courage and clarity. I am glad that you have decided to find your personal definitions along with me. As you embark on this journey of self-care, self-fulfilment and self-connection, you will find personal definition. Too often, as mothers, we become so involved with the cares, concerns and demands of others that we forget what we want.

This program was created to aid you in staying connected through your mothering experience and reconnecting if you have lost sight of you.

Practices:

Track your self-connection. Ask yourself the following questions daily, weekly and monthly to see if you are on track. There is no right or wrong choice. You know what you want to create from the assessment. Do your answers line up? If not, you have some work to do. If so, it is good for you! You are taking the time to get to know yourself again and maintaining that connection.

1. Self-connection is ______________________________.

2. I self-connect (once - twice - three) times a week.

3. I go to the ______________________________ in my home, office or ________________________ to self-connect.

4. I self-connect ___________ minutes for the day. My goal is ___________ minutes per day.

5. My idea of connecting with myself involves _____ ____.

6. I feel ______________________________ when I take the time to connect with myself.

7. Self-connecting daily has helped me ___________
   ______________________________________.

8. I spend _______ amount of time with myself each week.

Affirmation

I took an action for me today and it felt great!

____

(Your Signature)

____
____
____
____
____
____
____
____
____
____

CHAPTER 6

Finding Solutions

Moms are always looking for the best solutions to solve life's problems. As it relates to self-care, the greatest challenge is our own defunct ideology that says it's impossible to be a great mom and personally grow.

Recently, at a workshop I conducted in Atlanta, participants spoke honestly about their challenges in finding time, growing personally, finding connection, and sharing their Mom "Me" blueprint for self-accomplishing.

Many mothers admit they place their own unrealistic standards of perfection on their spouses, childcare providers and other support-givers. Do you share these tendencies? What unrealistic standards have you set that have limited the amount of support you can receive?

"It's not easy being a mother. If it were easy, fathers would do it" – from the television show, The Golden Girls

In addition, many mothers wanted to know how to let go everything that is bringing them down.

These mothers have been running on auto-pilot for so long that they don't know how to get out of the vehicle. They have a difficult time seeing what the other possibilities might be for their lives. Is this you?

As I listened to these mothers, I immediately thought what moms want are solutions to this very deeply emotional challenge of letting go in order to experience a new life. This chapter was created to give you some simple strategies to begin to create a new mindset.

To embrace a new perspective:

1. Raise your standards
2. Change your belief system
3. Change your strategy

Raise Your Standards

Anytime you want to make a change in your life you must raise your standards.

Write down a list of the things that you are tolerating. Tolerations are things that we may or may not choose to change, but it is important to articulate what these things might be.

Some examples of things you might be tolerating as a mom are:

- Unstructured bedtimes for the children
- Multiple meal requests at dinner
- Too many after school activities

Use your journal to detail your responses.

Mom-Me Assessment

Consider the following:

1. What are you tolerating?
2. How might you modify these tolerations?
3. What are the benefits of making this change?

Changing What You Believe Is Possible

As moms, we like to believe that we cannot take care of ourselves and still take care of our children. That simply is not true. We tend to believe self-care means that we are selfish and somehow neglect our children, another untruth. If you want to change your life, you have to be open to change. Many times, moms will experience the symptoms that can hinder – or trigger – change in our lives, such as:

Feeling run down
Depressed
Sadness
Sickness
Aches and pains

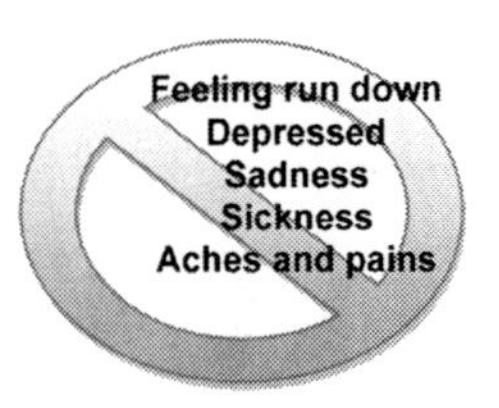

Making the decision to change will bring greater physical and emotional health.

Change Your Strategies

If we want to change our lives, we must change our old self-defeating patterns. We must begin by believing we deserve that which we desire. Many times we don't believe we deserve the very thing we are trying to achieve. Also, we have to stop tolerating the things that keep us from what we want.

Some of the things we are wrong to tolerate are: lack of respect and appreciation, lack of personal time, lack of boundaries, financial constraints and an unfair household division of labor.

Communicate deliberately. Learn to say no – decisively. If you can't do it, just say you can't do it, and leave no room for negotiating. All too often we say, *"I might, well, possibly, um, we'll see. I'll call you tomorrow."* It is unresolved and open-ended.

Instead, practice delivering closing statements looking in the mirror.

"No, I'm not going to be able to do that. Sorry."
"No, I'm not sure when I can."
"I'm sorry, but you can't bring her over today. It's not a good time."
"You'll have to pick her up by seven o'clock."
"You know, I'd love to help you, but that's not going to work."

Now you understand what you need to do to create the mindset for change in your life. Changing requires us to redefine our priorities.

The goal is to establish a personal vision and goals to complement that vision. Ask yourself what this objective requires of me, in order to accomplish it daily, weekly or monthly.

A terrific strategy to help moms create solutions in their lives and make room for accomplishing goals is to employ what I call DIPP.

DIPP Stands For: Delegate, **I**ncorporate others, **P**lan, and **P**urge

Delegate

Delegate some of your responsibilities to a spouse or your children. I have found when we are willing to ask the children to help make their beds, clean their rooms, put away the laundry, they are willing participants. We can be creative in teaching our children how to take age-appropriate responsibility for their things. Spouses are also more willing to help when they have some advance expectation.

1. What are some activities / responsibilities that you can delegate?

2. To whom can you delegate in your family?

3. What are some good reasons to delegate?

4. What are the benefits of delegating some household task?

5. What new possibilities will you have when you delegate a task?

6. How does your family benefit?

Incorporate others

Incorporate others in our space. Create a supportive network for yourself. This network can include friends, family, babysitters, and mother's helpers. Many times I have exchanged babysitting hours with a friend. My friend and I switch five hours each week. She watches my son for two and a half hours on Tuesdays and Thursdays, and I watch her child on Fridays so that she and her husband can spend time together.

What creative ways can you incorporate others into your space?

List the names of either people or services that you can add to your space. Some examples might include: friends, relatives, and mother's helper. *(i.e., 11, 12 or 13-year-old mother's helper could, for example, come over and watch your children to give you some time on the tread-*

mill. Or he or she could walk the dog with your kids. They would have fun doing it, and that very small task could give you a half hour or 45 minutes extra time for yourself!)

1. What type of support do you need?

2. Which of these resources of support are available to you right now?

3. What are the possibilities for you when using this support?

4. What are the benefits to your family?

5. What does your ideal support system look like?

Plan

Plan your days in advance. Look for ways to incorporate your pleasures into what you will be doing.

Will you be carpooling a lot tomorrow? How about taking along some of your favorite music, or a book on tape? Are you taking the children to the park to play? Then don't forget to take along a book to read so you can have a good time while they are. Pack a bag ahead of time for you – with your favorite snacks and things to do.

Plan each day at a minimum the night before. Consider the following:

1. What does your ideal day look like?

2. What resources are necessary for you to plan effectively?

3. What is possible for you when you plan?

4. What is the benefit to your family when you plan?

Purge

This is my favorite step. "Purging" is getting rid of the unnecessary. I used to drive my children all over the U.S. to baseball and soccer practices and gymnastics, until I noticed they didn't really *like* baseball, soccer and gymnastics. I realized when the sign-up sheet came home from school, I asked them, "You want to take soccer, don't you?" And they'd grunt, "Yeah. Okay." So we developed a new rule: If you want to do something, express yourself. Just tell Mom and Dad, and you can do those things, but if you don't bring it up, I'm not going to bring it up either. And it's not because I want to deny my children any kind of activity. It's because I have come to realize that not everything is necessary.

What can you get rid of in your schedule? What can you move to next week? Are there items on your list of things to do that could be eliminated? *(If it is not something that I need to do in the next 24 hours, then maybe it can be eliminated.)*

1. What can you eliminate from your day?

2. What are the personal benefits of purging this activity?

3. What are the benefits to your family?

4. What do you need to do to rid yourself of this life item? Make a call, or say no to extra-curricular activities.

When we practice DIPP we add more time and opportunity to achieve our goals.

Finally, here are some simple strategies that can help us find time for ourselves every day.

1. Renew your mind. Take some time every day to focus on something that makes you feel good. Eliminate things, events and people that drain your mental energy.

2. Journal your feelings. This is a wonderful way to keep a written record of your life. When I journal, I am often surprised by how much I am a creature of habit.

3. Create a book with pictures of your dreams, plans and goals, or use a board if you prefer. The goal is to give yourself visual reminders of the things you would like to accomplish. Some examples might be tickets to a favorite concert or lecture, or a picture of a book you would like to finish reading. Place your book or board in your connection place the place that you go everyday to be with you. Make it convenient.

4. Give yourself a break every day. Take a minimum of 15 minutes for yourself every day. This might require your getting up early or staying up later. It's worth it! You're worth it! Use this time to unwind and be empty. Don't think about anything specific.

5. Self-accomplish in mouse bites. Whatever you are trying to accomplish, remember that inch by inch it's a cinch; but, yard by yard it's hard. Take small steps toward your goals. The most important objective is to take small pieces consistently.

Some of you are saying, *it has been so long since I have thought about what I want.* What would give you a great quality of life? Start by asking yourself, what do I value? For example, I value quiet and reflection. As you clarify what you value, you will slowly be able to discover how to create peace within.

Maintenance

The objective of this book is to put you on a path to self-definition as mom. Just like establishing any routine, it is equally important to identify a maintenance routine to self-accomplish. I recommend the following:

1. Define a daily routine.
    - Visit your connection place daily.
    - Establish consistent times to plan daily.
    - View your daily calendar at a glance.
    - Keep a journal of progress.

2. Establish a mom-Me success partner
    - Identify five accountability partners. They can be friends or other moms you have met from our mom community boards or a mom coach. Visit www.timeformom-me.com or www.findingdefinitions.com.
    - Establish consistent meeting times to consult with your partner(s) or start a mom-Me Club. Go to www.timeformom-me.com for details.

- When you do these things you will become stronger than ever! (Not Neglecting Self)

Practices:

✓ Observe your physical appearance

1. Create a realistic wish list for change.
2. Record the things that you love about yourself.

✓ Date yourself

1. Write down five things you want to do alone.
2. Assign a date to accomplish these goals.
3. Journal your successes and obstacles.

✓ Dressing for success

1. Lose the mommy jeans.
2. Evaluate your wardrobe. Ask a fashionable friend for help
3. Purge anything you haven't worn in a while or is ill-fitting.
4. Plan your look.

✓ What is under your skin?

1. Schedule a complete physical yearly.
2. Visit the dentist yearly.
3. Visit the gynecologist yearly.
4. Follow-up with a specialist if you have any problems.

When you complete these actions you will be ready to Love Again. These are simple solutions that will help you find personal definition.

Affirmation

I took an action for me today and it felt great!

____

(Your Signature)

CHAPTER 7

T.A.K.E.C.A.R.E.

Now that you have experienced my program for creating a meaningful and fulfilling life, I want you to TAKECARE using my easy strategies for always considering your needs.

Here are some reasons why you need to T.A.K.E. C.A.R.E. of you

1. Your life matters. You don't have to wait until the children graduate from high school or start nursery school to do something for yourself. Start

today. Take small steps. Ask yourself: *What do I want? What do I like?*

There is a saying, "Never put off until tomorrow what you can do today," because if you enjoy it today, you can do it again, tomorrow.

That's exactly my point. Begin to enjoy your life today.

2. It is possible to self-accomplish and be a great mom. Dispel the rumors that moms can't be great for themselves and still take care of the family. It is simply not true. You can carve out a slice of your life and do something consistently for you each week. Consider having a massage or pedicure, meeting friends for lunch, or planting flowers in your yard. When we do something for ourselves consistently, we are renewed and rejuvenated.

3. Are you seeking a balanced life?

   Think about what it takes to balance on a balancing beam. First, you have to step on to the beam. Second, you must see where you want to go. Next, you will probably extend your arms to help you stay afloat. Finally, you begin by taking small steps until you arrive at the end of the beam. Balancing any aspect of our lives requires focus, consistency, a total commitment and perseverance. If you want a life that includes your family, spirituality, financial goals and personal passion, then creating balance is your only option. When attempting to balance your life, you have to get started and consider what you want to accomplish. Look at all areas of your day and take small steps until you get there.

4. Are you running on empty? Do you have more things to do than energy left to pull them off?

   Stop the roller coaster and understand that superwoman is not real.

5. Enhanced standards and expectations: elevate the way you live. Decide today you deserve the best.

6. Reduce Stress by learning to say "No."

7. Establish boundaries and work to enforce them.

T.A.K.E.C.A.R.E.

Time. Make time for yourself in your life. What are your dreams, plans and goals? What do you still want to accomplish? As mothers, it is so easy to make time for gymnastics, soccer, baseball and homework; yet, we forget to make time for ourselves. When was the last time you did something for you? How are you enriching your life? Are you fulfilled?

Take 15 minutes every day to connect with yourself. Start your day out with you. Take time to connect and hear your voice every day. Cut off the phone. Close the door, and take a minute every day to be alone with you.

Arrange your days. Plan your days in advance. When we plan our days in advance, we have a better opportunity to include ourselves in the day. Have you ever planned a great picnic lunch at the playground with your children during the day after a visit to a park, only to realize, upon arriving, that it would have been nice to have a book to read or some great music to listen to? As moms, we can include ourselves into our days by planning the night before. When was the last time you completed reading a book? Make the things you enjoy easy to access. Make your car your mobile university. Take books on tape with you in your vehicle.

Keep your life simple. Are you overscheduled? Do you find you are running your children everywhere and not able to enjoy the view? Why not? What is the race? Ask yourself, what activities can I eliminate from my life?

Evaluate your health. When was the last time you went to the doctor? I'm sure that most of you can remember when your children had their last doctor visit. What about you? When did you last go to your primary care physician or the dentist? I had a client – a well-educated mother of twins – who was shocked, upon visiting the dentist, that she had a broken tooth. She had never noticed that her tooth was broken. What about you? What do you need to learn about your body? How is your emotional health?

Create a supportive network. Establish relationships with friends, family, and mother's helpers. Outsource your laundry and housecleaning, if possible. Create opportunities to ease your workload to reduce personal stress and anxiety. Ask others to help you. Solicit the help of family members, friends and neighbors. Swap children with another mom you trust.

Arrange a date with you. Yes, you. Get to know yourself again. What are your hobbies and interests? What do you enjoy doing? Tell a story.

Relax every day. Give yourself a break every day. Stop the rollercoaster of life, and be still to hear your inner voice. Allot time in your days to relax at home. I suggest you create a quiet space in your home for relaxation and renewal.

Erase your need for perfection. You don't have to be perfect to have an enjoyable life. The house, your husband or your children don't need to perfect either. Give your life the needed flexibility.

Being a mom is signing up for a life of service, but not as a servant.

Are all of your family members helping with the housework? Arrange a meeting and coordinate the chores. Children under 10 should be provided with a list for checking off their to-dos. Many times a mother's feelings of being overwhelmed and under-appreciated are a toxic combination that will make her feel resentful over time. Teach your children to contribute to the family unit.

Remember Martha Stewart has a staff to help her create the wonderful creations that we see on television.

Remember you do matter and that your self-care is not negotiable, but necessary to be the best parent possible.

Affirmation

I took an action for me today and it felt great!

____

(Your Signature)

CHAPTER 8

Finding Tips

This bonus section was created as my gift to you. This is an assortment of newsletter articles I have written that will inspire you to change, using my simple strategies. Read and savor them, understanding that the key to finding you is simply taking small steps to discover a part of the whole you. Be sure to become part of my mailing list. Sign up at www.findingdefinitions.com.

Mom, do you know you?

Remember the song from the movie Mahogany? The song went, "Do you know where you're going to? Do you like the things that life is showing you? Do you get what you're hoping for? When you look behind you, are there no open doors. Do you know?"

This month, let's discuss your plans for your life. What are they? I bet if I asked you to tell me your family's plans for the month, you could come up with a host of activities. In addition, you probably know the list of to-dos that your spouse needs to accomplish as well. What about you? What are your plans? What are you going to do when you grow up?

Now is the time for you to answer these questions. As moms, we often forget to dream for ourselves. Many times we ride on the dreams of our husbands' and children's accomplishments and forget that we can dream the impossible dream for us. When we work toward a goal, it fuels and fills us. It gives us a new sense of purpose. Also, it sets the right example for our children – that we can self-accomplish and be nurturing and loving.

Have you ever said to yourself that you were going to go back to school or pursue a new interest when your child reaches that magical age? When that age arrives, you find that you have forgotten what it was that was once important to you. This is why as a mom you must not delay but must decide what you want to do with your life. Here are five steps to help you act today:

1. Write down five things that you want to do with your life. Remove all limitations, and dream big!

2. What does each of these goals require? (For example, to attend graduate school I might need to take evening or weekend courses, when child-care is most available from my family.)

3. List five reasons that you think this idea won't work. Answer the following questions for each:
   - How can this opportunity work?
   - What do I have to overcome to accomplish this? (Do you need child-care, financing, or is it plain motivation?)

4. What are the benefits? What will I gain by venturing into this new experience? Will I make new friends, learn something new, or expand my earning power?

5. Get your questions answered before making any decisions. Don't talk yourself out of what you want. Get all the facts first…then make an informed decision.

6. Take small steps toward your goal. Take one class instead of three. Start small for big results.

Fall: Moms! The Benefits of Making Mistakes

This month, I want to share with you the benefits of making mistakes. Many times as mothers we have every intention of doing a great job for our families. We read the best books to learn everything from how to get our children to sleep through the night to what the most important study habits of school aged children are. In addition, we plan healthy and nutritious meals to ensure our children's physical success.

Eventually, in motherhood, we fall. We make a mistake and forget something relevant or significant. How do you handle your mistakes? *Are you your own worst critic, or do you have hecklers?*

Making a mistake provides us with a new perspective and a set of information from a completely different vantage point. It is only when we pack the wrong items in our child's lunch that we come to know what the other possibilities are. Many times we continue to do things in the same old way, and we never have the benefit of seeing different outcomes. We can use our mistakes as learning opportunities to either get more information, to change unnecessary pressure from fixed routines, or simply to laugh.

Secondly, everyone makes mistakes. Erase your need for perfection and replace it with understanding. Understand that you are human, and that you are doing your best as a mom. Maybe you did put the baby's clothing on backward. This is insignificant in the big context of life. Maybe you missed the school play because you forgot to write it on your calendar. This provides you with any opportunity to discuss how moms – like kids – make errors, and when they do, they have to be honest and courageous about what happened.

Thirdly, surround yourself with people who affirm and support you as you grow in this stage of your life. Sometimes we feel the need to show others that we are really good at this life as mom.

Remember, that you have to do your best... not impress. Moms often ask me simple strategies to address others who question their parenting. I recommend the following steps to relieve this stress:

1. Establish some boundaries. Remember, we teach others how to treat us.

2. Ask clearly but politely that neighbors, in-laws, parents and friends who criticize and complain about your parenting style or approach give you some space. You might say, "What you said to me hurt my

feelings just now. I am learning and doing my best. You have to give me some room here."

3. Trust yourself. Know that your best is good enough.

Remember, that no one is perfect and that you don't need to be perfect to be a terrific mom. Being a good mom requires love, commitment and nurturing. If your parenting contains any combination of those adjectives then your mistakes are minor and your care is major.

Great Self-Care Equals Great Health-Care

How is your health? What do you do to stay fit on the inside as well as the outside? When did you last visit the doctor?

Parents are excellent at dragging their children to the milestone appointments. We call grandparents, aunties and friends to inform them how healthy the children are, or to tout their current height and weight stats. We celebrate our children's health as a tangible sign that we as parents are doing well by our children.

What about you? How is your health? Are you able to share your health story? Is your health picture one of success or neglect? As parents we have a responsibility to care for ourselves. We deserve to be healthy. Great health is a choice. We have the opportunity to choose every day to set the alarm one hour earlier in order to go on a walk. We can choose whether fast food is part of our daily health regime.

Some of the major causes of death, including heart disease, cancer, stroke, lung disease and injury, can be prevented through diet, weight loss, and exercise. While we cannot prevent all things that happen to us physically, we can slow down the aging process by fueling our body with the diet and exercise it needs to thrive.

As you think about your health? Consider your children. Our children are watching us. They are watching the example we set, whether it is a healthy example or one of neglect. What are your children learning from you? What we do speaks so much more loudly than what we say. What are you modeling for your family?

This month, make a commitment with me to apply some simple strategies to getting your health on track.

They are:

Schedule medical appointments with all of your doctors. This includes the primary physician, obstetrician/gynaecologist or any relevant specialist. Make your health picture crystal clear.

Establish a consistent exercise routine. Take a walk with the family after dinner. Rake the leaves with your children, and play. Make exercise fun! Start a walking club with moms in the neighborhood. If it is too cold to go outside, consider exercises that you can do indoors, like track, racquetball or walking n the mall.

Eat Healthy. Purchase snacks that are low in sodium and processed sugars. Instead, snack on healthy foods, like broccoli, carrots, apple slices. Preparing healthy meals together is a terrific way to create quality family time while educating the family on food choices. Create fun ways to eat foods that are high in fiber, fresh fruits and vegetables.

Decrease toxic activities, like drinking and smoking. It is a fact that one out of six deaths in the United States is blamed on smoking. Listen to your body, and minimize the harmful affects of tobacco and alcohol. Reduce your children's exposure to second-hand smoke.

Lose weight. Play when your children play. Find ways to make yourself move with the children. Park the car and walk to pick the children up at school.

Re-discover old hobbies. A hobby is a terrific way to become fit by doing something that you love. Join a softball league, yoga class, or swim team. Create healthy outlets for your health.

Being healthy is a necessity, not a luxury. Respecting your body and giving it what it needs will aid you in the long run. Change those bad habits into healthy choices.

Caring for yourself means caring about your quality of life. Remember that self-care is not negotiable, but necessary to being the best parent possible.

Moms! Don't Let Your Life Schedule You.

Do you define self-love as a selfish act that results in diminished care and concern for the other members of your family? When was the last time you treated yourself lovingly? What did you do for yourself?

Don't let your life schedule you.

Does the beginning of school have you stressed out? Have you found that since the start of school your children are sleepier than ever in the morning? Are your children slow moving and unable to locate the new supplies that you purchased for them for school?

You are not alone. Parents everywhere are dealing with the stress and anxiety of establishing back-to-school routine. For most parents, the routine unfolds slowly, although most of us have a plan of how the morning should run. The best way to reduce stress and anxiety is to establish a school routine as soon as possible. In addition, children always perform better when they know what to expect. I recommend involving your children when establishing the daily routine. It will take two to three weeks before everyone has adjusted to the new schedule. So start early.

My children enjoy summertime because it allows them the opportunity to sleep in and get extra rest. In order to get adjusted to the new routine, I rearrange bedtimes to reflect the school schedule three weeks before school begins. When school starts I recommend the following strategies for getting a family routine scheduled as soon as possible:

- Establish a nightly bed-time routine and stick to it. Small children usually perform better when rested. The American Academy of Pediatrics Guide to Your Child's Sleep provides some helpful guidelines regarding how much sleep children need at different developmental stages. These numbers represent the recommended total number of hours of sleep in a 24-hour period. So, remember to add those toddler naps into your numbers. They recommend the following:

AGE	HOURS OF SLEEP NEEDED
Birth-Six Months	16-20
Six-Twelve Months	14-15
1-3 Years	10-13
3-10 Years	10-12
11-12 Years	~10
Teenagers	~9

- Have them pack the book bags the night before. Make sure that the notebooks and all other school supplies are in the backpack to avoid frustration and the mad morning search. These unexpected events usually contribute to their being late for school and their parents for work. Teach children to check their book bags before they go to bed to make sure they have what they need. For younger children, create a check list of what the book bag needs for them to check off each day.

- Are you tired of making meals that no one eats? Take a family survey on the best breakfast meals that the children want to eat each week. This prevents parents from creating delicious meals that the children don't want to eat. Ask the children to collectively decide on five different meals for breakfast. Tell them that if they eat the food that they suggest then they can help plan the breakfast menu for the following week.

- Teach your children how to pack their own lunches. Children love taking ownership of their lunches. It is a wonderful way to increase the chances that lunch will be consumed instead of trashed.

- Prepare your dinner in advance. Bulk cook on the weekends and freeze dinner for each day of the week. This will give you more time to hear those back-to-school stories.

- Bathe younger children at night to avoid morning hassle. Lay out the clothing for the next day so that children can dress themselves upon waking up. For the finicky child, select two outfits so that he or she can have a choice in daily attire.

- Put a family calendar on the fridge that allows you to list all upcoming teacher meetings, orientations, meet and greet occasions as well as special events for the children. At the beginning of the school year, it is difficult to remember the different activities because they are all so new. Having a calendar will ensure that family members know what is going on and when, so no important dates are missed.

- Minimize extra-curricular activities until things calm down. This is tough to do but helps reduce anxiety and stress. It is difficult for a parent to pick a child up from school, have a quick dinner and then go straight to baseball practice.

- Commit some family time to having dinner together each week. Teach the children the importance of quiet and reflective time together as a family. Create a time after dinner to share important highlights about each day.

- Parents, minimize your stress by being proactive and creating a plan. Taking the time to schedule your life will prevent your life from scheduling you. Remember that self-care is not negotiable, but is necessary to be the best parent possible.

Moms! Exercise Choice In Your Life.

Are your self-care muscles weak? Do you suffer from indecision, complacency or the whatever-you-want syndrome? Do you pass up opportunities for yourself because you are afraid to simply commit.

This month let's talk about the benefits of choice.

I love coaching moms! Specifically, I love helping mothers realize their dreams, plans and goals. As a coach I have found that most mothers are challenged with giving themselves the green light to live their lives. Is this you?

Perhaps you have a group of neighbors who walk together in the morning who want you to participate. Or, maybe you want to take an evening pottery class for your enjoyment. What's stopping you?

Most moms create a list of reasons why they should not choose to do the things that add value to their lives. As moms, we can easily create a list of more important things to accomplish.

I want to encourage you to put yourself at the top of the list. Your family wants you to be happy, healthy and fulfilled!

This month, e-mail me your commitment story. Feel free to write one sentence or two. I want to know what your plans are for you.

Here are my four tips (using the acronym for **L.I.S.T.**) for exercising choice in your life.

L List 10 things that you want to accomplish (e.g., exercise, make a new friend, or pursue a hobby or passion).

I Investigate your options. Many times we fail to pursue the things we love because we do not have enough information. Find out the times of that aerobics class. Get in touch with an old friend to schedule lunch. Get your questions answered.

S Stop making excuses and start making connections. Ask yourself, "How can this work?" Look for the possibilities to create the opportunities that you want.

T Take time to live your dreams daily! Pursue your passion.

S.U.M.M.E.R.

Moms, are you ready for the summer? What plans have you made for your family? This newsletter is designed to give you some ideas of how to make this the best summer ever for your family.

Here are my seven strategies for making the most of **S.U.M.M.E.R.**. They are as follows:

Send out invitations to arrange play dates for the children and social get-togethers with family and friends. The summer provides terrific opportunities to catch up with long lost friends or family members. Take some time to create a list of people you want to see this summer. Invite them over for a cookout, a visit to the pool, or coordinate a joint family vacation.

Uncover easy and simple things to do at home with your family. Blow off the dust from your family board-games and play them instead of storing them. Remember the sprinkler in the backyard? Turn on the sprinkler for the children and take out umbrellas to use as shields. Children love this type of water-play. Look for easy ways to have fun at home. No gas or cash necessary.

Move every day. Take a walk through your neighborhood or visit a local park/playground. The American Heart Foundation recommends that we take a minimum of 10,000 steps a day. Look for easy ways to move together as a family. Have a family jump rope competition or volleyball match. Write down five ways to move together as a family. Encourage family fitness while having fun.

Make reading a part of every day. Visit the local library and have the children select three favorite books to read over a two-week period. Every day give your children time to read independently (including the picture readers) and also read a story to your children every day. Children who become fluent and strong readers usually do so as a result of others' commitment to read to them. (Moms, while your children are reading, read for yourself.)

Eat well. The summer is a terrific time to modify diets to include all of the wonderful summer fruits and vegetables. Set a goal to eat a minimum of one fruit or vegetable at every meal. For example, at breakfast you might prepare a fruit salad with pineapple, strawberries, honeydew and blueberries with granola. At lunch you could serve raw broccoli, celery and carrot sticks with a light sandwich. With dinner, you could make a spinach, walnut and apple salad. It is really that simple.

Reorganize your home. Clean out those closets and purge the unnecessary. When de-cluttering, create bins for things to keep, things to donate, and things to get rid of. Do you have a collection of toys that are unused? Give your children the opportunity to donate those unused items to a family shelter. Help reduce clutter in your living environment.

My strategies for **S.U.M.M.E.R.** will aid you in having a meaningful, productive and healthy summer for all. Enjoy!

Self-Care for Parents

The demands of family life are exhausting. Carpooling, school activities, and birthday parties are just some of the many things we support in our children's lives. As parents, it is easy to become so inundated taking care of our children that we forget to nurture ourselves. This month, let's make a commitment to nurture Mom and Dad. Our children are counting on us to set the right examples for them to follow. Let's teach them the value of self-care. By doing so, we illustrate to our children the importance of loving ourselves.

When we take time to care for ourselves, we feel empowered and are better able to accomplish more in our lives. Caring for ourselves permits us to love everyone around us better. As a result, we become more giving, grateful, and happy. By establishing quality adult time, we can connect and reflect on who we really are and what we really want. When was the last time you considered what was best for you? When was the last time you relaxed in your favorite chair and enjoyed a cup of coffee? How many minutes each day do you get to connect with your spouse? Making the commitment to improve the quality of each day is a decision. Take small steps to enhance your life.

Over the course of this year I am going to share with you some specific strategies on caring for Mom and Dad. As the mother of three children between one and eight years old, I know first-hand the challenges that parents face. My husband and I make time every month to consistently nurture ourselves and our relationship.

I believe that the best parents are ones that place their self-care as a priority. The benefits to our children are immediate when we take better care of ourselves. By sowing self-care into our lives we reap the benefits of reduced personal stress, anxiety and frustration.

This month, follow my five strategies for Renewing the Self:

Rest

Find time to be still every day. Take the time to stop the roller-coaster of life and slow down. When we are rested, we make better decisions.

Read

Renew your mind. Fall in love with reading again. In my home, we Drop Everything And Read (D.E.A.R). Set clear expectations with your children that everyone is going to read individually for 15 minutes, thereby limiting interruptions. No excuses. Reading allows us to escape the pressures of the day and allows us to expand our minds.

Rejuvenate

Rejuvenate your spirit. Take some time each day to connect with your higher power. Pray, reflect and meditate to connect with your spirit and allow peace to work in your life.

Readjust

Readjust your priorities. Is your family too busy? This is a great question to ask. Is your family racing from Monday morning to Sunday evening? Limit your children's activities. Be realistic about each commitment.

Reward

Reward yourself. Go on a date with yourself, your spouse or a friend. Take some time away from the children and enjoy some grown-up time. When you return you will feel like a new person.

Making the decision to care for yourself is a choice. This month, choose to make self-care a priority. Remember that self-care is not negotiable, but necessary in order to be the best parent possible.

Self-Care for Parents II

Is your life balanced? What does that mean?

Do you often say, "There are not enough hours in a day" or "I just wish I had more time"? If you have answered yes, then this may be a sign that your life is out of balance. How do you find balance in your life?

The symptoms of being out of balance are feeling

rushed, hurried and anxious as you take on the daily events. When we are out of balance, we find it difficult to enjoy life. Many times poor scheduling dictates the quality our lives. Instead, we need to build a life that reflects our values and priorities. I do believe that it is possible to have it all in a lifetime, but not necessarily at the same time.

What are your obligations and responsibilities? Balancing our lives comes in many different sizes. For one parent finding balance might mean increasing the ability to let others help out, delegating tasks to others or perhaps finding services that can ease day to day responsibilities, such as a pick-up and drop-off laundry service. For another, family balance might mean identifying ways to coordinate the challenges of work with the demands of finding quality family time.

As for me, balance means living a life in accordance with my values. It means making time every day for solitude, family and my personal passion. By prioritizing my time according to the things that I value, I create a life that is abundant. Because I am clear about what I value, my priorities are my litmus test for what I should do next. Balance to me means that I create opportunities to delegate the unnecessary and purge the ridiculous. What about you? When are you at balance?

As parents, it is very easy to become so busy that you forget to hone in and consider what is most important. Here are my seven strategies on balancing your life:

1. Delegate. Create a weekly meeting with your family to discuss household responsibilities. During this time, review household responsibilities and delegate age-appropriate chores. Hold the meeting during the same time each week, and review what is working and what is not. For children under the age of 10 years, provide a goal chart so they can check off each task for accountability.

2. Consider outsourcing the laundry, grocery shopping (there a many grocery stores that deliver) or basic yard work to create more opportunities for quality time.

3. Plan your life. If you want to have days filled with less anxiety, you are going to need to plan in advance the activities of the family, work and other significant items. Planning allows us the necessary time to adjust and be proactive about the choices in our lives. This reduces stress and anxiety.

4. Eliminate what is not working. Look at ways you can add time to your days. What can you live without? Do the children have to go to gymnastics this

semester if you have a particularly heavy work load this quarter? Be reasonable.

5. Seek quality not quantity. Identify five activities that you enjoy that take very little effort. Incorporate a movie night on Fridays. Have the movie delivered to your door; add some popcorn and a pizza. This is a wonderful way to have both a quality family event and add no additional stress to your days.

6. Give yourself a break. Be reasonable. Are you trying to work all day, come home to make dinner, clean the dishes, get baths going, read night-time stories , clean the house and pay the bills in the evening? Ask yourself, is it possible to accomplish any of these items another day?

7. A great way to reduce stress is to exercise. Take a walk with your family three times a week for 20 minutes.

Understand that balance means limiting the things that are the source of anxiety and frustration. By adjusting our lives according to our values and priorities we make room for the things that allow us to enjoy life.

Question: What is self love?

Self-love is an understanding that caring and accepting oneself provides healing. Just as we express care for our children when they have an interest, a hurt, make a mistake or fall, showing ourselves the same understanding provides us room to grow. When we express self- love, we refuel our spirit and refresh our life. Make room for yourself to finally take cooking lessons or to enrol in that aerobics class. Remembering what you love is a great starting point.

Five simple strategies to show yourself love this month

Make yourself a priority! Choose to place yourself at the top of your list of things to do.

Choose an activity for you. Along with scheduling gymnastics or swim class for the children this month, schedule a massage for yourself. Perhaps you could take time to have tea with a friend, take a short walk after dinner or join a book club.

Write yourself a love letter! Take some time and review what qualities and traits you like about yourself. Begin your letter with: Dear__________, You are......

(Be sure to use words that describe your personal attributes.)

Schedule a check up. Place your health at the top of the list this year. When was your last medical appointment? Are you healthy? Do you have important medical questions? Let's get them answered.

Take a long bath weekly! During the evening, schedule a long bath with yourself. Remember to plan ahead and bring a favorite book, music or special fragrances that invigorate you. Check out www.MomSelfCareProducts.com to see the products I recommend.

Place something beautiful in your home just for you! Light your favorite candles or buy yourself flowers this month.

Challenge: During this month keep something beautiful that you love in your life daily.

Again, don't forget to sign-up for my newsletter (it's free) at www.findingdefinitions.com.

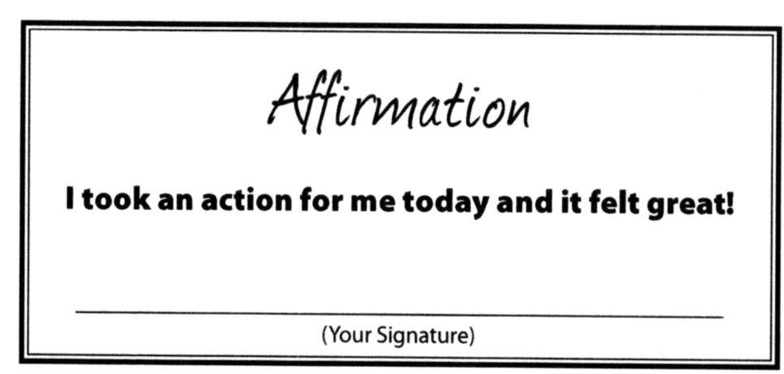

In Conclusion...
The Next Steps

Now that you have read my book, I would like you use this journal section to record some of your personal goals, insights, solutions or favorite tips. Let's call this your "cheat sheet" to ensure that you remember what works best for you.

Review each chapter and record a personal discovery that you made regarding each chapter's strategy.

For each chapter ask yourself:

- What shift can I make today in this area of my life?

- What is my next step with my own self-care?
- What routines or rituals work best to keep me on a successful path?
- What are my self-care goals?
- Why are these goals important to me?
- How would my life be more fulfilling if I address this area of my life?
- How would my family benefit?

- What are the steps I must take to ensure my own self-care?
- What is the timeline for this goal?
- How can I use the DIPP strategy?
- How can I break this goal into smaller pieces?

Also, remember to join our Community Forum for moms. There you will find mothers just like you, looking for solutions to this life called motherhood.

Thank you for committing to your own success.

Live Fully,
Mia

About Mia

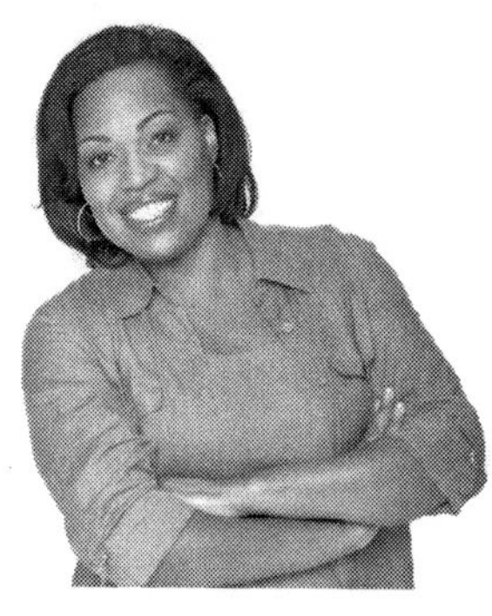

Mia Redrick, The Mom Strategist, is a best-selling author and a popular speaker.

Mia has reached thousands, both nationally and internationally with her empowering message for moms that states "self-care is non-negotiable but necessary to be the best parent possible." Mia's goal is to empower one million moms to practice better self-care.

As the founder and CEO of Finding Definitions, LLC, she is leading the charge to establish self-care groups for moms across the country using her turn-key system.

Mia's book, *Time for Mom-Me: 5 Essential Strategies for a Mother's Self Care* is a best seller on Amazon. She is co-author of *Taking Time to Care for Me: A Nurse's Guide to Self Care.* Mia is the National Time for Mom Examiner and the Parenting Examiner for Examiner.com as well as a featured contributor for Twittermoms.com InspireMeToday.com, SelfGrowth.com and MommyTalk.com. She was a columnist, for Family Digest Magazine with her column "Parenting is No Joke". Mia has been featured in The Washington Post, Women's World Magazine, CNN. Com, Paper Dolls Magazine, Modern Babies and Children, and the PG Gazette. She contributes parental traveling tips to the Home Away Traveler International Newsletter, which reaches 95,000 homeowners around the world.

Mia is a dynamic speaker with an personal story and an amazing ability to inspire the expert in every mother. She was featured on Sky Radio's "Conversation for the Expert Segment," which airs in more than 29,000 North Western American Airlines flights. She has appeared on ABC News "2 The Point", The Darla Shine Show, Family Talk Radio, Real Money, National Public Radio (NPR) Tell Me More with Michel Martin, Women Ready for Change with Dr. Karen Gail Lewis, Fabulously Successful, a French podcast, with Dawn Bournard and more. Mia co-hosted Team Radio on

WOLB 1010 AM Radio and is a local Parenting Expert for ABC News 2 in Baltimore.

Mia's work has been recognized and awarded numerous government citations. Redrick received the 2009 Women Helping Women Award from the Soroptimist International and has been recognized by The Maryland General Assembly, Official Citation 2009, U.S. Senator Benjamin L. Cardin, Certificate of Recognition 2009, United States of America, Member of Congress – The Honorable John P. Sarbanes, Certificate of Special Recognition 2009 and the Baltimore County Council Resolution Honoree–2009 for her amazing work in empowering women.